W9-BEM-251

HIDE:

A Child's View of
the Holocaust

NAOMI SAMSON

University of Nebraska Press

Lincoln & London

Library of Congress Cataloging-in-Publication Data
Samson, Naomi, 1933–
Hide : a child's view of the Holocaust / Naomi Samson.
p. cm. ISBN 0-8032-9272-4 (paper : alkaline paper)
1. Samson, Naomi, 1933– . 2. Jews – Persecutions – Poland.
3. Holocaust, Jewish (1939–1945) – Poland Personal
narratives. 4. Jewish children in the Holocaust – Poland
Biography. 5. Poland – Ethnic relations. I. Title.
DS135.P6S254 2000 940.53'18'092–dc21 [B] 99-37498 CIP

This book is dedicated to the memory
of my beloved mother,
Fanny Sorgen (Faiga Rosenberg)

CONTENTS

Foreword

As the survivors of the Holocaust age, it has become more and more critical that their stories be recorded for the sake of generations to come. That is what has energized the Spielberg Foundation to conduct its thousands of interviews. That and other reasons have led many individuals to tell their stories.

Any telling has value, deepening the record and belying those in future generations who would deny the horror. And, in some way, if the telling serves the need of the teller, then all to the good.

It is, however, particularly valuable when the one telling the story has a true talent for writing. That is the case with Naomi Samson, the author of *Hide*. I was introduced to Naomi and her husband, Harry, through a friend. Naomi, aware of my association with the Anti-Defamation League (ADL), immediately told me that she was a Hidden Child and had attended the ADL's historic Hidden Child Conference in 1991. Naomi began telling me something about her experiences, and I was moved and impressed by her articulation and sincerity. She soon brought me a manuscript she had written about her life as a Hidden Child. Several days later, I picked it up and did not put it down until I was finished reading it.

It is a powerful document, not only because it is an incredible tale of survival but because Naomi has the unusual skill of letting events speak for themselves. As a result, readers feel as if they are living the events with the family rather than reacting to commentary on the events.

One element that comes through dramatically in *Hide* is the dichotomy between the clear lines of good and evil on the one hand and the complexity of human behavior on the other. Naomi's direct way of presenting her material allows readers to see very clearly the evil of those perpetuating the Holocaust as well as the innocence of the victims. At the same time, complexity abounds. Those who protected the family are the most diverse people – from true heroes to those who are calculating and looking out for their self-interest even while doing good to those who are so calculating that betrayal is inevitable.

And there is, as well, the complexity of the victims. Naomi's family is a wonderful, protective unit, but they are real people who feel anger and guilt as well as love and care.

Hide is a memoir to remember, and I am honored to have been involved in its publication.

KENNETH JACOBSON
Assistant National Director
Anti-Defamation League

Preface

My mother's story, printed here, is not only a recounting of her memories but also the culmination of a lifelong struggle to live with them, a struggle that did not neatly end when the war was over in 1945. Although they were liberated from the Nazis, in the bodies and minds of its living victims the Holocaust lived on like a parasite of remembrance. They lost not only their loved ones, their possessions, their homeland, and their community but a part of their souls as well. The survivors live with these demons every day of their lives, and therefore it is with great awe that I view my mother and wonder how she has managed to cope with these lasting memories, these terrible images, these heart wrenching losses. Of course there were lingering nightmares and flashbacks, and every *yahrtzeit* (anniversary of a loved one's death) carries her back to that dark, tormented place again and again. For a survivor almost any moment can remind you of it. Eating a piece of bread at dinner can transform you into that starving little girl who would have fought like a wild animal for a morsel of food. You pass a person in uniform in your neighborhood and suddenly you are surrounded by Nazis, staring down the barrel of a machine gun.

My mother's battle with the Holocaust demons has been long and arduous. For a long time the world did not want to hear the survivors' stories. There were times when her struggle with sadness and fear almost overwhelmed her. But she fought this fight as well and bestowed upon me, my brother, and my sister the love and nurturing of a devoted and caring mother, a strong and courageous mother who persevered and gave to her children when there was little left inside of her. She gave with her heart, although her heart had been broken. She gave with her soul, although her soul had been robbed. She led us down the road to adulthood with unconditional love and encouragement and without bitterness, guilt, or resentment. My mother was tough when she had to be and taught us to stand up for ourselves and what we believed in. But most of all she was compassionate, helping others in need, offering a bag of groceries or lending an empathetic ear to a recent immigrant, neighbor, friend, or stranger, as well as to her family.

I will always be indebted to my mother for sharing her story with us. She will always feel some anger, some fear, but through her life, her survival, her story, we can all rejoice in the redemption of a lost soul, the mending of a broken heart, the resurrection of a tormented spirit, the gift of life, and the promise of a new generation.

My mother did not live in biblical times, but to me the great plagues pale in comparison to her experiences. My mother did not walk in the time of Pharaoh or Haman, but to me the evil force that hunted her was of demonic proportions. And yet there were no miracles, no manna from heaven, the sea did not recede and lead her to safety. To me this is greater than a miracle. She had to summon her courage. She had to find the will to survive, to continue to run and hide, and to fight to live. It is for this courage, this strength, that we her family and all whose lives she has touched will be forever grateful.

JOSEPH SAMSON

HIDE

After three years of humiliation and slow torture by the Nazis in Poland – with the help of many Polish gentiles – life for us, the Jewish people, was rapidly coming to an end. Cities and towns were now being emptied of Jews. The German word *Judenrein*, which means "cleansed of Jews," was heard more and more often. Jews were being sent to camps by the masses, never to return. People were constantly looking for places to hide, to run away from the frequent "roundups" for deportation. The atmosphere was thick with gloom and fear. Forgotten by the rest of the world, we, the chosen people, it seemed, were now chosen for torture, humiliation, and finally death at the hands of the murderers.

One of the darkest days in my life was November 2, 1942. The night before, as in the previous couple of weeks, my mother had dragged us children down into our hiding place through a trapdoor in the kitchen floor, because *Judenrein* was inevitable. The SS, the Gestapo, and the German soldiers, with the help of many Polish collaborators, would usually attack at night, killing many Jews on the spot and rounding up the rest for the camps.

"No more hiding," said my oldest sister, Chaya-Leeba, on that night. "Don't you all see? It's no use – we cannot escape an army and so many willing Polish people who are eager to help point out the Jews. So why not die with some dignity, the way Father taught us before they killed him three weeks ago? Daddy was a great man, and I will soon join him."

With tears in her eyes, my mother took the rest of us kids down – my two sisters, Perele and Janice, my brother, Josh, and me. I was the youngest, nine and a half years old. At dawn Mother said, "Well, it seems we may be safe for another day," and we came up and closed the trapdoor.

This old house in the town of Frampol, Poland, was full of people, including us, who had fled from many places. We had fled originally from the town of Goray. As each of us started finding his or her nook on this cold November morning, we were all shocked to hear and see trucks full of Germans with helmets and machine guns. Wasting no time, they jumped off the trucks as they were still moving and began shooting at the Jewish people at random, yelling, "Get over there! Line up, you cursed Jews!"

People started to scramble. Pushing, shoving, trying to run away from the rain of bullets. There was so much confusion and so little time to think which way to run. While still near the house, we had to step over people who had been shot. They were screaming and begging for help. Young women on the ground, bleeding, clutching their babies, were crying out for someone to help them. But none of us could afford the luxury of giving these poor souls even a few seconds, because all of us were in the same situation.

Soon we reached the gentile section of town, but still there were fierce-looking German soldiers with machine guns chasing after us. By this time it seemed that they had a planned pattern. They knew the areas where the Jews would try to escape, and they surrounded those areas. We ran through the mud and jumped over fences into the fields, which were freshly plowed and very difficult to run in. My mother kept shoving me over these high wooden fences, and I kept getting weaker from being thrown over and falling on the ground. At one point I realized that my mother was quite a distance away, my sister Perele was also ahead of me, and they were the only people from my family now running near me. My only thought was that I must not lose sight of my mother and Perele, or I'd be dead and they wouldn't even know where I died. In my panic I screamed at the top of my lungs, "Please, Mama, please, Perele, don't leave me here alone to die!"

Mama couldn't hear me. She was a little farther ahead than Perele. The shots and the screaming of so many wounded people were deafening. Perele heard me and slowed down so that I could run with her. Our hands kept pulling apart, so she said to me, "Hold onto my coat pocket, Naomi, our hands are slippery."

As I grabbed hold of her coat pocket, I caught a glimpse of my mother, who was still running ahead of us. She would turn for a second and motion to us to hurry up. There were so many people running, falling to the ground screaming when bullets would hit them. The sound of the machine guns, held by those fierce-looking Germans with helmets on their heads, was unbearable. As we kept on running, we came upon more wounded people on the field and more dead bodies that we had to step over. The wounded were whimpering and begging for help. Several times on that day I would be faced by helmeted Germans about to shoot me, but by sheer luck the machine gun would be turned away from me toward a bigger crowd. Suddenly, Perele fell to the ground. I fell down with her, thinking she wanted those Germans near us to think we were dead. Then she said to me, "Dear one, I've been hit by a bullet in my leg, I can't run anymore. You, child, get up quickly and catch up with Mother."

"You get up!" I yelled at her with anger, as if to say, What are you doing to me? "Get up and run with me!" I yelled again.

"I can't anymore," she said, "but you, Naomi, you can still run, so waste no more time. Maybe someone from our family will survive to tell about these horrors; maybe that someone will be you." And she pushed me away.

I remember turning my head back toward Perele while running again, this time alone. I hesitated for a moment, thinking, "What should I do now? Should I die now, near Perele, or continue until I'm shot and killed?" I hoped I wouldn't just be wounded, to die a fearful death out here in the muddy field, the way Perele and so many others were now dying. Perele lifted up her head and waved at me to continue running. I saw her right hand touching a body lying by her side. Her face was flushed; she looked so beautiful. What did her words, "survive to tell about these horrors," mean? No one would survive that day, especially not little me. No more thinking – I had to continue to run.

Now the ground was covered with many more people, and fewer were running. The shooting was still fierce, and I ran on with all my might. Suddenly, at a distance, I saw my mother! "Mama, Mama!" I cried.

At first she couldn't hear me. Everybody still alive was screaming something. Most people were calling to God, begging for help.

I, too, was crying to God, "God, what is happening today? Is this the end of the world? Please help me!"

Finally I caught up with my mother, and she took my hand.

By this time it was late afternoon. We couldn't see any more Jews or Germans, but we could still hear some sounds of gunfire. We kept on running, only more slowly. After a while we began to see a village, houses that gentile people lived in, and children playing games and singing songs, like my friends and I used to do. My mother ripped off her armband with the blue star of David on it. I was panic-stricken. "What are you doing, Mama? You know that Jewish men and women have to wear an armband with the Jewish star, so that the Germans can easily identify us, and if you take it off and they catch us ..."

"It doesn't matter anymore, child. Jews are no longer permitted to live, with or without an armband," replied my mother.

With a sinking feeling in my stomach, I turned to my mother and asked, "Mama, how come these children are playing games and are not afraid of being killed, but I am?"

"Don't talk so much," said my mother. "Keep walking a little faster."

"Mama, look at those girls. They are just like me. They are playing skip-rope and other games and singing the same songs my friends and I used to sing when we were still allowed to live. Why are they free to sing and play, while I have to keep running and hiding from the Germans?"

"You know why, child. You are Jewish and they are not," said Mama. "Walk a little faster, Naomi, or we'll be dead a lot sooner than you think."

"But Mama, what's wrong with being Jewish? You and Daddy always taught us that to be Jewish is to be good to others, to be considerate of other people, to say my prayers to God every morning and every night. I have been doing just that, and I never hurt anybody. I'm only nine and a half years old, and I haven't had much time to do many good deeds. Why then, Mama, must we die only because we are Jewish?"

"I don't know, child. Don't ask so many questions. We are not supposed to question the Almighty. It seems he decided our fate. No more questions, just keep walking as fast as you can."

Then Mother said, "We have to get into the forest, because these children's parents might drag us into town to be killed by the Germans so that they can collect a bag of sugar for each of us. That is the reward the Germans are giving to help clean out Jews." (At the time I couldn't quite comprehend what she meant, but it became clearer to me about three months later, while in hiding. We learned that my mother's only sister and her husband were found hiding, and they were brought into town tied up with rope for the Germans to kill them. The two village boys who brought them in were rewarded with two bags of sugar.)

I stopped asking questions and walked along with Mama until we were deep in the woods and it was quiet at last. But the gunfire was still ringing in my ears, and the expressions of pain and fear on people's faces were still with me. Now we stopped.

"Let's lie down," said Mama. "We seem to be safe for now." My mouth was dry and hungry, my lips parched. Exhausted from this long day, I lay down on the ground very close to my mother. She put her arm around me and I felt her squeezing me tight as I fell asleep, pretending our nightmare was over. But our nightmare was to go on and on for two more years.

The early morning sun was piercing through the almost naked trees as I awoke and tried to open my eyes. As I tried to move away from my mother, all parts of my body were aching. My mouth and throat felt dry and painful, and my lips were chapped, but I managed to sit up. My mother didn't move. Her eyes were still closed, and her face looked very sad. I touched her a few times, and finally, she sat up.

"Mama, what will happen now?" I asked. She just looked at me with sadness. "I'm hungry, Mama, and I'm also aching, and I'm cold. What are we going to do now, Mama?"

Again my mother looked at me sadly, and tears came running down her cheeks. "I don't know what we are going to do, child," she said. "Our whole family is probably dead – they were all killed. All the Jews we knew are now most likely dead. It's just you and me here in the wilderness. I envy the dead. They do not have to die again the way you and I do."

I panicked as my mother again talked about dying. "But Mama, we don't have to die, we can live right here in this forest forever. I'll never complain again." I was shivering as I looked at Mama. She drew me close to her, and we both wept uncontrollably for some time. Then my mother noticed some wild berries in the distance. She pointed her finger toward them and told me to go get them. I picked for a while, but then I realized that my mother must also be hungry, so I picked a handful of these berries and brought them to her. I spent the rest of the day looking for more berries. There weren't many berries left in November, and I was scared to go too far away from Mama – we mustn't lose each other in the woods.

Late that afternoon my mother said that when it got dark we would leave the forest and try to reach the village of Zagrody, where a family by the name of Chmelinsky lived. Mr. and Mrs. Chmelinsky had some of our valuables that my father had entrusted to them to keep them safe from the Germans. Mother said that he was an honest and decent man. "Maybe he will help us."

"That's great," I said. "We are not going to die, after all!"

My mother started looking around, trying to figure out which direction was the right one for the road to Zagrody. When it got dark, we started walking. It seemed we walked forever before we saw the houses of the village of Zagrody. My mother knocked on the window of Mr. Chmelinsky's house several times before he came. He opened the window, looked at my mother and me, and then crossed himself. "What! You are alive, Mrs. Rosenberg? And this is your girl?" He asked.

"This is my baby girl, Naomi. She's hungry and cold. Please, Mr. Chmelinsky, help us hide somewhere. You can keep our belongings. Please do it for this child's sake. She is scared to die, and she has really not lived very much."

I stood there and prayed to God that this man would have pity on us and help us.

"Wait right here. I'll be out in a minute." He walked away from the window, and I saw two of his daughters, about my age or so, standing with their mother's hands on their shoulders. How I envied them! When he returned, Mr. Chmelinsky led us into a barn packed with hay. He told us to push ourselves in near the wall as much as possible, and he said, "I'll be back soon."

We pushed away the hay as much as we could and sat down. He returned with a pitcher of milk and a chunk of bread. We gobbled it up in no time. While we were eating, he took his lantern and disappeared. "Let us say our nightly prayers," said Mama. We said the *Shema* together in the dark. We felt so grateful for this nook in the hay.

But it didn't last. At dawn, while Mama and I were sound asleep against a wooden wall, Mr. Chmelinsky started shaking us. "Get up!" he yelled. He handed us winter clothing from our family's hidden belongings – my brother Joshua's herringbone coat for me and a wool shawl for Mama. Then he told us we must leave.

"Please, please," we begged him. "You don't have to feed us much," said Mama. "We will be no trouble to you. Just let us stay, and we'll be very quiet. No one will ever hear us."

"Get out immediately," he said, "or I'll kill you myself!" And he pulled a gun from his jacket pocket. "I'm not going to risk my life helping Jews. Out – fast!"

He pushed us out of there and told us never to come near his property again. As my mother cried and begged some more, he pulled the trigger and we heard a shot. Each one of us thought the other one was wounded as we ran with all our might. We realized that he was serious about killing us if we didn't leave him alone.

Once again we were in the woods, sitting on the ground watching another day begin. With my brother's coat on me and with Mama now wearing her woolen shawl, I was more hopeful that my mother would think of another good plan to survive. "Mama, what will we do now?" I asked.

"Tonight we will try another village, called Zastavia," she answered.

When the sun went down once again, my mother had to decide which way to go out of the forest to get to Zastavia. When we got to Zastavia, Mother once again knocked on the windows of people she had known for years. In one house a young woman came to the window, and when she saw us, she yelled to her husband, "Żydy [Jews] – get up and kill them!"

We ran as fast as we could, then hid behind someone else's house for a few minutes. When we were able to catch our breath, we continued. But we ran into more and more bad luck. Finally, a gentile woman opened her window and gave us a bowl of cold potato soup, which we ate in no time. When my mother asked her if she would hide us, she quickly responded, "Mrs. Rosenberg, you and your little girl are Jewish, so you have to die. But we will not risk ourselves in helping Jews. Jews must die now, not us."

With that she grabbed back her bowl and shut the window. Near her house was a large haystack. My mother got an idea. "Let's try climbing to the top of this haystack and covering ourselves with hay." It took us a long time to climb up, but we made it. While we were climbing up that mountain of hay, I saw the woman staring out of her window, watching us. No sooner did we get settled than we heard someone crawling up after us. "Well, once again it's the end," I thought. It was the woman's son.

"Hey, Jews, let me take you into town to the Germans and I'll get a bag of sugar for each of you. You know if we help find Jews we are rewarded with sugar and sugar is hard to come by. You will die anyway."

"Get down from there, and don't you have a hand in killing people!" yelled his mother. "Let others clean out the Jews!" Then she shouted, "And you Jews get down and run or I will let him kill you right here!"

Needless to say, we ran with all our might until we found ourselves in the wilderness once again, this time in the middle of the night. "Mama, what are we going to do?" I asked once again.

My mother was quiet for a long time. I looked at her face to see her expression. It was a dark night with few stars in the sky. The trees were tall and there were so many of them. They made me think of the German and Polish guards who had surrounded our hometown ghetto in Goray for the past three years. Suddenly, my mother spoke. "Listen to me, my child," she said. "We can't go on like this. We will either die of starvation and the animals will eat our flesh here in the woods, or someone in these villages will kill us. I have decided we should walk to our hometown, Goray, which is about eight or nine miles from here, and give ourselves up at the Jewish cemetery. That way we will be buried with other Jewish people."

"No, no!" I cried. "I will not die this way or any other way! I want to live, Mama, I don't want to feel bullets fired in my head or body! Bullets are hot and they burn a person's insides and it hurts badly until the person is dead!"

"Don't think about that part," Mama said. "Think about heaven and all our family. We'll all be together. Think about your friends, your sisters and brother, all the people in our town who are waiting to greet us in heaven. Think about that."

"No! I will not be killed! I refuse to die, Mama!"

"Stop crying like a baby. I can't take it!" said my mother.

So I got up and I walked away from her and sat down with my back against a tree trunk. I was angry at Mama, but I was even more frightened now, because I sensed that my mother's mind was made up.

The next day was just as hard as the day before. I looked for berries, but there were few. I was cold, thirsty, and hungry, and oh, was I scared! But, most of all, I was now very angry with my mother. We didn't speak all day. At night we tried again to get some help, but time after time we experienced the same bad luck. Either people tried to catch us and bring us to the Germans for sugar, or they just tried to kill us on the spot. This went on for several more days. And every day Mother talked about that cemetery in our hometown, Goray, and I wouldn't hear of it.

At one point I told my mother, "Go get killed at the Jewish cemetery the proper way. I'll stay here by myself."

"You can't," she said. "Don't you understand, child? We can't escape a whole German army, plus the Polish people who are helping the Germans wipe out every last Jew."

"But, Mama, this war will end and the Germans will lose, Daddy said so many times."

"That is true, Naomi. The Germans will lose, and they will suffer and pay for all the horrors they are causing now. But we can't outlast them and survive."

For about four or five more days, I kept fighting for life with Mama, while every day we grew weaker, colder, and more thirsty, but less hungry. I would put wet leaves on my lips and tongue to suck up the dew. Finally, I too thought that death was the only way. So with much fear and sadness, I turned to my mother and said, "Let's go and die with some dignity at the Jewish cemetery in Goray."

It was a cloudy afternoon, and a thin snow was coming down when Mother and I, hand in hand, started walking toward Goray. It seemed to me we walked for hours. No one bothered us. I, wearing my brother's coat, and Mama, covered with her shawl, must have looked like any other mother and child. I had no more fear in me, no more feelings either. We just kept on walking.

Suddenly my mother stopped. "Look, Naomi," she said, pointing to some houses off the road. "This is the village of Lada. We used to have many gentile friends in this village. In this first house straight ahead live the Kowaliks. Dear friends. Let's stop in to see the Kowaliks. We have nothing to lose anymore," said Mama.

So we got off the road and walked straight toward their house. It was getting dark outside. We walked into a hallway that led to the door of the Kowaliks' kitchen. My mother just opened the door and walked in. When Mrs. Kowalik saw us, she yelled out loud while crossing herself, "It's you, Faiga Rosenberg! You, you are alive! You are not a ghost are you?"

"Yes, Maria Kowalik, I'm not a ghost yet, and this is my youngest daughter, Naomi. Can we sit down?" asked my mother.

"Sit, sit!" she answered.

It was warm in her kitchen, and the food on the stove smelled so good! Four of her seven children were in the kitchen, staring at us, as Mrs. Kowalik brought over some milk and bread. "Eat and drink. You both look awful," she said.

As I ate the bread, I was thinking of how we would soon be killed at the cemetery, and the food just wouldn't go down my throat. My mother was telling Mrs. Kowalik that we were the only ones alive now from all the Jews in Goray.

"No, you are not the only ones. Two days ago your sister and her husband were here, and I fed them too."

My mother's face came alive. "What, my only sister, Hudel, and her husband are alive? Where are they? Are you hiding them, maybe? Please tell me!"

"No," said Mrs. Kowalik. "I sent them on their way like I'll ask you to leave now, too. I can't risk my family to save Jews. It's a terrible war!" And then she opened the door and asked us to leave.

As we walked out of her house, I expected that my mother and I would continue our walk to Goray to our death. But instead, my mother said to me, "I have an idea. Don't ask any questions. Just stay with me and do what I do."

Mama took my hand, and quickly we walked toward the Kowaliks' barns and stables, about three hundred yards from the house. There we crawled under a wagon near a wall and sat down. My heart started racing again with hope. But I kept quiet. About two hours had gone by when Mrs. Kowalik came out with a bucket to milk the cows. Mama pulled me by my hand and we went over to her as she was milking a cow.

"Jesus Christus!" Mrs. Kowalik yelled out. "You keep scaring the life out of me! What are you still doing here? My daughters, Wlatka and Juzefka, will be here in a minute to help me milk the cows, so you'd better be on your way!"

"We have no place to go to," Mama said. "If you don't help us hide, we are just going to give ourselves up in Goray to die. Our lives are now in your hands, Maria Kowalik. Please don't have this child's blood on your conscience. Please hide us somewhere here!"

I stared up at Mrs. Kowalik's elongated face, praying she would have pity on us. She looked down, then looked at my mother and said, "All right, but only for one day." She put a very long ladder up against a trapdoor in the ceiling of one of her barns and told us to climb up after her. The barn loft was almost filled with hay, which was winter fodder for her animals. She helped us pull out lots of hay until we reached the low part of the gable roof. There we made enough space for Mama and me to lie down. As Mrs. Kowalik left us, she said, "Don't forget, this is just for one day." Then she pushed more hay toward us to create a wall of hay to the top of the roof, so that if anyone would come up they wouldn't see us in our hiding place. "Don't talk to each other in a normal voice," she said. "Whisper."

I didn't let myself think about tomorrow. I thought, "Maybe today can last forever." I just curled up against Mama and fell asleep.

But tomorrow came, and Maria Kowalik came up too. This time she brought us a pot of potato soup. Her daughter Juzefka, who was about seventeen, came with her. Juzefka helped her mother pull down the hay, and they appeared with the soup. "Eat this soup," Mrs. Kowalik said, "but tonight I want you out of here."

So the begging began again. This time my mother put her hand in her bosom, came up with some money, and handed it to Mrs. Kowalik. "Take this. There will be more money and other valuables for you if you keep us here."

"Where are you going to get more money and things?" Mrs. Kowalik asked.

14

"You know Mr. Saverek Zlomainsky?" my mother replied. "He has many of our things, and money too. You know he is a great and kind gentile, and we Jews trusted him and gave him money, jewelry, and other valuables to hide while this war lasts. He will surely give me back things for you if you keep us."

"Well, maybe two more days. When will you go to see Mr. Zlomainsky?"

"Tonight," replied my mother.

"Good," Mrs. Kowalik said. And she and Juzefka built up the wall of hay and disappeared, taking the long ladder away.

"Good," I thought. "There is hope now after all."

That evening Mother and I worked diligently and quickly, pulling out hay in one area against the wall. We made a hole so that my mother could climb down the barn wall to go to Mr. Zlomainsky. She told me to be very quiet and not to answer anybody until she returned. Our signal would be for her to cough twice and then call, "Helena," which was now my official Polish name.

This was the first time I had been left alone. I started thinking, "What if my mother gets killed? Mrs. Kowalik will surely throw me out, and that will be the end of me. What if my mother just doesn't come back to me? After all, it is easier for her to hide out alone than with a young child. Children are big problems. What if Mr. Zlomainsky kills my mother?" Panic filled me. The time passed so slowly that it seemed forever.

While these gruesome thoughts were running through my mind, I heard Mother cough twice, then say, "Helena?" She'd come back! Gingerly, she climbed up that high wall, and I helped her into our hiding place, covering up the hole again.

"Oh," she said, "Mr. Zlomainsky was glad to see me alive, and he gave me money and a gold pin to give to Mrs. Kowalik. He said to tell Maria Kowalik that if she keeps us, he will see her in church on

Sunday and will talk to her periodically and give her more money discreetly." This way my mother wouldn't risk her life – and he would not risk his for being seen with a Jew.

"Tell Mrs. Kowalik," Mr. Zlomainsky had said, "that the war will end pretty soon. The Americans will soon be pushing from their side, and the Russians are getting stronger and will rid the Nazis from this side forever. Tell her I said so. She knows I know politics."

Oh, was I happy that night! Imagine, there was hope that we would survive and live forever and ever! Now my mother was saying she could start looking for her only sister, Hudel, and her sister's husband, Mailach.

But Maria Kowalik, scared, kept up her daily speeches to us. She would point out to us how no one else would let us in their door, let alone hide us for even one day. On this day, she was furious with us. "I'm not going to risk my life and my children's lives in order to save Jews," she said. She looked very angry as she spoke. "If my husband, Jozef, were alive today, he would have never allowed this to happen. You would not be here now. So go, get out of here!"

"But Maria, we have no place else to go except to our death if you throw us out," pleaded my mother.

"Yes, yes, you keep on saying this about your death all the time in order for me to have pity on you. But no more! Tonight I want you out! You hear me – out!"

I shivered, my teeth were chattering, and that panic was all over me as I listened to Mrs. Kowalik speak. There was silence for about two minutes, and then Mrs. Kowalik continued in a somewhat softer voice, "And suppose I made a big effort to keep you here and by some miracle you did survive this awful war, what will happen to me when I get to heaven? You are Jews, and Jews are Christ-killers. How would I justify saving Christ-killers who crucified and killed our Lord Jesus?"

16

"But Maria, even if this is true that the Jews killed Chr——"

"Even if it is true? You know it's true!" she interrupted my mother, looking angry again.

"All right, Mrs. Kowalik," said Mama. "What I mean to say is that we, today's Jews, had nothing to do with the killing of Jesus. That happened a long, long time ago. About two thousand years ago. How can we today be held responsible for what happened so long ago?"

"But you see, Faiga, you Jews will always pay for his crucifixion. You will always be responsible for killing our Lord Jesus."

Once again, there was a pause as this tall, skinny woman, dressed in a gray cotton dress down to her ankles and a kerchief tied under her chin, stared at me with her pear-shaped, stern-looking face. When she saw Mrs. Kowalik looking at me, Mama took the opportunity to say to her, "But Maria, we are human beings, aren't we? And when you save a human soul, the Lord rewards you. Your daughter Marinka is about the age my Helena is, they could even pass for sisters. Their coloring is the same. Blonde hair, light eyes, fair skin. And both of our daughters are human beings. So you see, I feel that by saving human beings you will be rewarded in the hereafter."

"I suppose so," replied Mrs. Kowalik. "You are human beings." And with that, she turned and disappeared down the long ladder.

Several days went by without any further hassle or long conversation with Mrs. Kowalik. She would bring us some food daily and would empty our toilet dish every couple of days.

One Friday night about twelve days into our stay in our hiding place, Maria Kowalik came up, turned to my mother, and said, "Listen, Faiga, two of your children were in my house earlier today. Your son Joshua and your skinny daughter."

"What! Two of my children are alive? Where are they?"

"I gave them some food and wrapped their bare feet with rags. You know there is snow on the ground. Then I sent them away," said Mrs. Kowalik.

"How could you send them away? Why didn't you bring them here to us!" shouted my mother.

"Keep your voice down, Faiga. I couldn't do that because I won't be able to keep you either," she replied.

"But for now, how could you send them away? My only son and my daughter Janice! We could have been united for now. How could you, Maria?"

"Well, you see, Faiga, my husband's brother Stanislov was in my house, and you know how he feels about Jews. So you see, I couldn't do that and let him know that I'm hiding Jews."

Mother and I were stunned and bewildered as Mrs. Kowalik went down the ladder. Mama came close to me. She touched my arm in the dark and said, "Listen to me, *mein kindt* [my child]. From now on I will have to leave you here alone every night and go knocking on people's doors, searching everywhere I can, until I find your brother Joshua and your sister Janice. Now, Naomi, can you stop shivering and show me how brave you can be?"

"Yes, Mama, I'll be brave."

When the next day came, all I could think of was how Mama would leave me alone at night to go look for my sister Janice and my brother, Joshua. As soon as it got dark, Mama said to me, "Remember our signal when I return. I will cough twice, then call out, 'Helena,' and you will pull away the hay against the wall to open the passageway. Lie quietly, and don't make any noises."

"Mama, I'm scared," I said.

"Yes, I can see you are scared," Mama answered, "but I have to go, so calm down and let's open the passageway against the wall."

And so we did. I watched Mama climb down the high wall under our loft that was packed with hay. I looked down as though I'd never see her again. She looked up at me and scolded me for not closing the passage fast enough. She said that I was not being a responsible person and that any wrong move I made would cost me my life. So I closed it up very fast, and I couldn't stop shivering from fear – as I am shivering right now, so many years later, reliving the past as I remember it so very clearly, so very vividly.

I decided that I had to do something to stop having these gruesome thoughts about losing my mother. All I could think of was that someone was killing her, or that she found a place to hide out by herself because I was too much trouble. Children were nothing but trouble now, and nobody wanted us. All these horrible thoughts were controlling my mind. It overwhelmed me to a point where all I could do was put my face in the hay, bring my knees up to my chest, and cry. Remembering what Mama had said about not making noise, I tried to cry without making sounds. And while in my internal hysteria, I began to fantasize.

I started seeing my girlfriends' laughing faces. There was my friend Leah Hut, the leader of our gang. There were Chana, Rochele, Mayta, Chaya, Hinda – and of course there was Yochi (Yochevet). Yochi was the most fun to play games with. She was always hugging us all and always giggling. Her laughter was a pleasure. I could hear her even as I was thinking about her. There were also Wanda and Junia, our Christian friends. Now we were all playing games. Playing hopscotch, jumping rope – and, yes, we were playing hide-and-seek. We were also making mud pies and cookies. A moment of reality made me think and wonder how each of these girls met with death. No reality, back to fantasy and games and fun. Lots of fun, fun . . .

"Helena, Helena, can you hear me?"

Oh, it's Mama, her signal! She's giving me the signal to open the passage.

"What took you so long, Naomi? I thought maybe someone had killed you, you didn't answer for a long time. Did you fall asleep?" she asked.

"Sort of," I answered her. "Tell me, Mama, did you find Janice and Josh?"

"No, I didn't," she said. "I was in eight houses in this village so far. Some of the villagers tried to kill me, others just shut the door in my face, telling me to get lost. You know there are about a hundred and twenty houses in Lada, and all these farmers have a lot of land. There's a lot of walking between some of these houses. At the last two doors I knocked on, the people were especially angry with me because I woke them. How dare I? They don't like to be awakened, especially by a Jew. Tomorrow I'll go again as soon as it gets dark."

And so it went for the next five nights. Mama would leave me and I would try to think of pleasant things to distract me from being scared. Often the pleasant thoughts would fade and the unpleasant ones would take over. I would think of the so-called good old days when we were still allowed to live in my hometown ghetto. Even though those were bitter times and we could see the end coming, we still had some hope.

Nineteen forty-two was a most difficult year. It had gotten progressively worse since the war started in Poland on September 1, 1939. In 1942 it was quite common for German soldiers to burst into Jewish homes and demand more reichtung (valuable possessions). By that time the Germans had many gentiles in town who would tell them which Jews were well-to-do. Some of these gentiles took on a double role, however. One man, who pretended to be my father's friend, helped my father hide some fur pieces in the backs of our dining room chairs. Two days later the SS slammed open our doors and went straight to our dining room. They turned the chairs upside down, pried off the sheets of wood, and removed the fur pieces. After yelling and threatening, they took the furs and left. Sadly, at this point my father realized he could not trust most of his gentile friends anymore, so he no longer called on them.

One Friday afternoon in the late summer of 1942, four SS men came bursting in, confronted my parents, and in loud and strict voices demanded the reichtung. My father gave them some money from a drawer and a pair of his gold cufflinks and told them that we had very few valuable possessions left. "Your people have completely exhausted our belongings," he told them.

"If we find anything more that is of value and you have lied to us, we will line you and your children up against the wall and shoot you! Understand?" they shouted.

They began to pull out drawers from furniture and turn them upside down on the floor. They swung their rubber hoses and broke several cabinets. They swung the hoses at our china closet and broke it and everything in it - smashed and scattered on the floor. Some old vases and other glass things that had been in the family for generations now lay broken on the floor. They even shoved the pots, with the food that Mama had scrounged for all week in order to have it for the Sabbath, off the woodburning stove and onto the floor. They emptied everything onto the floor and looked for whatever they were looking for - gold, maybe diamonds? They didn't say. Now they decided to search all of us. They looked in our hair, in our clothes. They ripped down the hems of our skirts. "You Juden have tricky ways to hide things," one of them was saying, staring at me.

I wanted to tell this big uniformed man that they had taught us well. And who did they think they were? And what gave them the right to our belongings? We were hiding *our* things – things my parents had worked hard for. They were just here robbing us. I felt like screaming and biting and scratching their eyes out. But all I did was what they dictated, because I was very frightened.

They continued throwing and smashing things to the floor. Then they hit the big grandfather clock on the wall. As the clock came crashing down, it broke in pieces, and money fell from the hiding place in its double bottom. The SS men were outraged. "How dare you, *Juden*! You lied, you will all die!"

My mother, who was sitting on the floor, jumped to her feet and started to talk to them. "Dear sirs," she said. "Please, listen to me! You've got to believe me. This money belongs to my brother-in-law, who is doing *zwanks arbeit* [forced labor] in the town of Yanov this week. He put the money there, but I never told the rest of my family about it. They knew nothing about it. He will be back from forced labor next week, so you can verify it with him."

"*Ach, du cursed Jude*, you are always lying to the Germans," shouted one of them. "Line up. You will all be killed!"

By now, we all knew the strategy that might be our last resort. We all fell at their feet, kissing their boots and begging: "Lieber Herr, bitte schenken sie mir das leben! [Please spare me my life, dear sir!]," we cried. And as we all begged in great hysteria, they were swinging their rubber hoses at us over and over and shouting all kinds of obscenities at us, the Jews. But somehow, once again, it worked. They warned that this was the last time that they would forgive us. Then they left.

Late that night, after we had managed to pull ourselves together and had cleaned everything up, Mama put the little food back on the stove, and we all sat around the table, which was covered with a white cloth in honor of the Sabbath. When my father started to chant the *Kiddush* (the blessing over the wine), Mama broke down and cried. She wept bitterly and kept asking why this was happening to us. Daddy tried to comfort Mama by telling her that Hitler would lose the war and that as long as we managed to be alive and together we would be the winners. "Let them take all our material things, as long as they let us live," he said.

But Mama said that we had so little left by now. With tears running down her face, she was saying, "What gives them the right to humiliate us so much and scare us and our children? Why, we barely escaped death once again today!"

Daddy agreed that Mama was right. "But as long as we are all alive and together right now, that is all that matters," he said. "I would let them have all our possessions even for our youngest and littlest child, Naomi."

My adrenaline jumped to the ceiling. What did Daddy mean, "Even for our littlest Naomi?" Why *even* for little Naomi? Did that mean that I, little Naomi, was not as important as my older siblings? Just because children and old Jews were being killed more often. My fears were overpowering. They were consuming me. I decided that I would have to look out for myself, because everybody was nervous, everybody was scared.

Many terrible things were happening in 1942. My friends and I liked to play in the sandbox. That was always lots of fun. We had to be careful, though, to remember to be home at 5:30 P.M., the curfew for Jews. One afternoon in August, late that day, my friends went home one by one - all except Chana and me. We got carried away building castles in the sand, and we forgot about the curfew.

Suddenly I heard a loud bang, as if the world shook! Chana fell face down into the sand. She turned around, looked at me, and made some sounds. I put my hands on her head, wanting to ask what had happened to her. When my hand came up red with blood, I realized that she had been shot.

I looked up and saw Stefan Mrożyk on his balcony, a rifle in his hands. He was pointing it at me now, and I knew who shot Chana and who would be shot next. So I left Chana to die and ran with all my might toward our house as Mrożyk fired bullets at me. Unharmed but breathless, I arrived at our door, where Mama was waiting for me. She dragged me in, shouting at me for forgetting about the curfew. Didn't I know that Stefan Mrożyk had become a full-fledged Polish collaborator and had had the Gestapo swear him in as one of them so that he could help them against the Jews? Mrożyk and his gang were very helpful to the Germans. Mrożyk not only handled a lot of the Jewish affairs for the Germans but also had a hand in sending many of his own Christian politicians to concentration camps.

The next day we had to bury Chana – Chana Stein, my friend, murdered. She was only nine years old.

Akzias (attacks) against the Jews were now taking place more often. The old and the very young were rounded up and put on wagons. They were driven out of town several miles, usually into the forest, where they were each shot and killed, then buried together in mass graves. My brother Joshua and I would always be hiding out, together with our two sets of grandparents, and would be told to come out when it was safe. People were also dying from sickness due to unsanitary conditions in the ghetto. But I was still living at home with both of my parents, my brother, and my three older sisters.

These were some of the memories going through my mind while I waited for Mama to return from her search for my sister Janice and my brother Josh. I dreaded the way she would return, exhausted and sad, with no sign of finding Janice and Joshua. But on the sixth night, amid my fears and panic, I heard my mother cough twice (our signal), and by the way she called out "Helena?" I sensed good news in her voice. While crawling up the wall to our hiding place, she was saying, "Yes, yes, Naomi, I found them! I found them alive!"

We closed up the passage tightly, and Mama hugged me and told me how once again she had almost given up the search that night. Then she entered Mrs. Sosnowich's house. After getting over the shock of seeing Mama, Mrs. Sosnowich revealed that she was hiding Janice and Josh and another Jewish fellow from Goray, whose name was Shlomo. Shlomo was about nineteen years old. Mrs. Sosnowich, her nineteen-year-old daughter Zosha, and Mama walked together for awhile until they came to Mrs. Sosnowich's barns and stables.

"Go ahead, Mrs. Rosenberg, you and my daughter Zosha can crawl under this barn to get to the hiding place of your children and Shlomo. I'm too big to get under this floor."

Mama, who was thirty-nine years old and quite thin by now, crawled under this floor. She scraped her wrists and knees. She was bleeding, but she didn't complain. When they got to the spot, Zosha knocked on a board above her head and said, "Żydy [Jews]." A board opened, and Zosha told my mother to climb in. "I'll lie here and wait for you. There isn't enough room in there for both of us."

"Inside it was pitch black," Mama told me. "I knew that they couldn't see me, only hear me. So I called out their names. At first they froze, unable to believe it was really me. Then Shlomo said, 'Mrs. Rosenberg?' And the children said, 'Mama, it's you, it's you!'" Josh and Janice hugged and kissed her in the dark and cried from joy.

I listened to Mama telling me all of this, also in the dark. "Mama," I said, "Maybe Mrs. Sosnowich will take us in, too, so we can be together. And anyway Maria Kowalik keeps on threatening to throw us out all the time."

"No, child, don't even think it. Mrs. Sosnowich already asked me where I was hiding and if I could take the three of them with me. She said she had pity on them, so she took them in, but it's getting more and more difficult to keep them. So, knowing the situation here, I lied to her. I told her that I was with the resistance group, the Partisans, in the woods and that they don't allow young children. But I whispered to Janice and Josh and told them where we are."

Mama was quiet for awhile, then she said, "If the war doesn't end soon, they will probably get sick and die in that hole."

I asked Mama to describe their hiding place to me.

"Well," she said, "there is a barn full of hay packed very tightly from floor to ceiling. Something like here. They opened a board under the floor and pulled out some tightly packed hay and created a sort of cave, enough for the three of them to sit or lie down on some hay. They must have worked very hard to create this cave where they eat, sleep, urinate, and maybe more. It smelled awful in there. Hardly any air gets to them through the floor. Zosha complained that she crawls on her belly every day to bring them food, and it's very hard to do that. So you see, I had to tell Mrs. Sosnowich that I will bring her something of value next time I come. I also told her that the Partisans predict that this war will be over very soon and that she will be rewarded for her good deeds. Now, Naomi, let us say our nightly prayers, the *Shema*, and go to sleep."

My mother never told Maria Kowalik about the nights she went looking for my sister Janice and my brother Josh. She said that Mrs. Kowalik must not know that Mrs. Sosnowich was hiding them or she would insist that we go to Mrs. Sosnowich too. Mrs. Sosno-wich, of course, thought that Mother was in the woods with the Partisans.

"So, Naomi, this must remain a secret," Mama would say. "These are bad times, and we have to lie in order to survive. Both of these families find it difficult to hide Jews. Jews are no longer allowed to live. *Judenrein* is everywhere," Mama said sadly.

And so it went for the next several weeks. We stayed hidden in this loft filled with hay, and every day we would hear Mrs. Kowalik complain to us and say, "Go, get out, I can't feed you! Food is scarce. We're in a bad war. I can't risk my family because of you Jews, so vanish, disappear, just leave my property!" And Mama repeatedly told her that we had no place else to hide and that we could get by with very little food.

One evening in mid-January 1943, Mrs. Kowalik came up the ladder with our food for the day. By now I could recognize her tone of voice, and I knew that she had another sad story about a Jew caught and killed. Hearing these stories, I always feared that this would also happen to us.

She started by saying, "Remember Isaac Pfeifer's daughter, Riv-ka? Well, she was killed today by the SS in Goray. She was eighteen years old. Lucky they never found out where she was hiding. She never stopped screaming until they shot her in the head, so they couldn't interrogate her. Had they been able to ask her questions, I pity the people who kept her until now."

Then she asked us again to leave by morning. She didn't even wait for another plea from Mama. She just climbed down the ladder, closed the trapdoor, and left.

About an hour later, while Mama and I were silently lying down, we heard someone moving in the hayloft and getting closer to us. I grabbed Mama's hand as we lifted our heads.

"Mrs. Rosenberg? Faiga? It's me, Pesach Pfeifer," came the voice in the dark.

Pesach was Rivka Pfeifer's sixteen-year-old brother. He was frightened and talking loudly as he came over to us. We could barely see him, but we heard him very clearly. "Hush," said my mother. "Don't talk so loud."

Pesach said that he heard Mrs. Kowalik tell us about how his sister Rivka had been caught and killed. Now he was all alone. He told us that both he and Rivka had been hiding in the same long hayloft as we were, only at the opposite end. When they first made their own hiding place here, he told us they intended to ask Mrs. Kowalik's help with food. But because they could hear and even see a little when Mrs. Kowalik would come up and bring us food and could hear how she always asked us to leave, they decided to stay quiet. Every couple of nights, Rivka would go begging the village people for food. When she returned, he would help her climb up the wall, just as my mother used to climb up and down when she was looking for Janice and Josh. Now Rivka was dead, and he was scared. He was also very hungry, so he had to stay with us, he said.

"Are you out of your mind?" said Mama. "You did hear how Mrs. Kowalik threatens us all the time. I can just see her face when she sees another Jew up here!"

Pesach was wild. He kept moving around and speaking loudly. "You will keep me here! I'm not leaving you!" he insisted. "Better give me something to eat. I'm famished and scared."

I was crying quietly, thinking it was all over for us. I visualized Yanek and Bronek, the Kowaliks' oldest sons, physically throwing us out and maybe even beating us to death so we wouldn't tell the Germans where we had hidden. I just couldn't believe this was happening, now that I had built up some kind of hope. In the dark all I could see was a flicker of light here and there. I held on to my mother's arm, and I felt her trembling. "Mama, what are we going to do?" I asked.

"Nothing, nothing at all!" yelled Pesach. "You will stay right here, and so will I. If you go somewhere else, I will go with you!"

He kept rambling on and on. Mama was quiet and squeezed my cold hand. I could sense the sadness in her. I could feel her agony in trying to make some kind of move. Then she spoke. "I'm thinking of some way to save this terrible situation. If Mrs. Kowalik sees us all here, she'll be shocked and have us killed somehow, without anyone ever knowing. On the other hand, if I go to her house by myself and explain things to her face to face, maybe she will have pity on us and keep us here. And you, Pesach, will have to learn to be quiet and go hungry without complaining, just the way we have been doing. And then I will come back here," said Mama.

I was crying again, begging Mama not to leave me here alone with this wild boy. But Mama said that this was our only hope. So down the wall in the dark my mother climbed. Pesach took off his scarf and said to me, "I'm going to tie your right arm to my left arm; that way you can't run away from me in case I fall asleep. As long as I have you with me, I know your mother will return."

I kept on crying and telling him that I hated him. Why did he have to come into our lives now? And why didn't he just go away? As I was crying and talking, he fell asleep. But every time I moved even slightly, he woke up and yelled at me and called me a bad girl. I never fell asleep that night. I just waited for my mother to return. Finally, I began to see daylight peeking through the little openings in the roof, and still my mother was not back. I heard the Kowaliks coming to feed the animals and milk the cows. By now I knew their morning routine.

When I tried to untie the scarf, Pesach woke up, shouting at me very loudly, calling me crazy, and warning me not to try this again.

Mrs. Kowalik pushed the trapdoor open with the ladder and yelled out, "Hey, what is going on up there?"

I pulled him over with me to the opening. When Maria Kowalik saw Pesach and me, she crossed herself and said in an astonished voice, "Jesus Christus! Helena, let me see your mother right away!"

"My mother?" I asked, surprised. "Isn't she in your house?"

"What are you talking about, crazy child?" she said.

Suddenly my whole world collapsed. Now I was sure that my mother had deserted me in order to save her own life. "I'll never see her again," I thought. "I'm as good as dead, or worse, I still have to go through death - and I don't want to die!"

Now Pesach was untying the scarf, and Mrs. Kowalik was ordering us to come down the ladder. Pesach kept holding on to me for dear life - or death. He kept telling me that my mother would come back and that as long as he had me he had a chance to live. He said that I was his only hope.

Down in the Kowaliks' courtyard, I again asked Mrs. Kowalik about my mother. "Are you sure my mother didn't come to your house last night?"

"Your mother never came to my house, Helena."

"Can you hide us?" asked Pesach.

"No, I can't!" she shouted.

She took some milk from the bucket that Juzefka was milking into and gave both of us a drink. I was in such shock I couldn't drink. She asked me what happened, and I told her the whole story about Rivka and Pesach and about Mama's promise to come back. She listened quietly, and tears appeared in her eyes. But then she said to us, "Now, children, go. May God watch over you."

She led us out of her courtyard and closed the very tall doors. Outside the Kowaliks' grounds I felt forlorn, alone for the first time in my life without my mother to protect me. I really felt that I might as well die. So I started walking toward the road to town. "Where are you going?" asked Pesach.

"To Goray to be killed and buried at the Jewish cemetery," I replied.

"You little idiot, they will kill you and . . ."

"Yes, Pesach, they will, and I know. I want to die," I whispered.

"You can't die. Your mother will come back for you, you'll see!" He started pulling me back, and I fought him. "Leave me alone. I want to die! Go, try to save yourself. You'll soon find out that there is no way for a Jewish child to be saved. And anyway, it's all your fault," I said.

"My fault? My sister was killed. What can I do alone? Nobody will hide me, a Jewish boy, you know." Then he was pulling and dragging me in the snow back toward Lada.

"Go away!" I shouted.

"No, I will not go without you," he said.

Then we were fighting – me hitting him with my fists, and he slapping me in the face and kicking me – really fighting, until we both fell flat in the snow. Now I was angry, really furious. I got up, and with all my might I started to run away from him. In the distance I saw a house, and I ran toward it as fast as I could go.

When I finally got there, Pesach was far behind me. I started to knock and bang on the door, yelling, "Please open the door for me!"

The door opened and a village woman looked at me standing there out of breath. "Parshiva Żyduvka [Filthy Jewess], go away!" she said, and she slammed the door in my face. By now Pesach had caught up with me.

"Come, let's go back to the Kowaliks. Maybe your mother is back for you now." Exhausted as I was, I dragged along with him.

Mrs. Kowalik saw us in the courtyard but didn't say anything at first. She just ignored us. Then she started looking at Pesach and said, "You could go into the forest near the town of Yanov. They say that the Partisans use young Jews to do work for them. Maybe that way you might survive."

"Are you saying that I should go and you will keep her?" he shouted.

"Not at all," she answered. "I'm talking to both of you. Neither of you can stay here, and what other - or better - options are available to you?"

She kept on mentioning the Partisans in the woods until at one point Pesach said to me, "Maybe we should try our luck in the woods with the Partisans. It looks like your mother left you for good after all."

It was sometime in the middle of the day; I was lightheaded, sore all over, disappointed, and disillusioned. I just couldn't think straight any longer.

"Come," he said.

I had started to walk with him, when he turned to Mrs. Kowalik and asked her to bring down his few belongings from his hiding place up in the hayloft. "Go get them yourself," she replied. "Here, I'll put up the ladder to the opening so you won't have to climb up the wall on the other end, and you can get all your belongings."

"Oh, no," he answered her. "I'll go up and you'll let Naomi get away, won't you? Her mother may come back after all. I've got to hold on to her."

At this point, Maria Kowalik grabbed me and sat me down on the window ledge of the horses' stable. She took off my shoes and stockings and threw them way into the stable and then said to Pesach, "Fine with you now? She can't go anywhere in this snow barefoot. Right?"

"Fine," he said, and he climbed up the ladder.

As soon as he was in the attic, Mrs. Kowalik ordered her son

Olesh to take away the long ladder and put it up against the barn wall all the way on the other end of the courtyard, nearest to her house. She told Juzefka what to do with me, and she told Marinka to get my shoes and stockings out of the stable. Juzefka grabbed me and carried me to where the ladder was now, and while climbing up, she said to me, "We are trying to save you, so be very still and don't ask questions."

She worked very hard and very quickly once we were up in this new barn loft, pulling out the yellow straw right up to the roof gable. She put me down where the roof met the ceiling and said to me, "I'm going to cover you with straw, but you will be able to breathe, so don't fret. Just be very quiet, and don't move at all." And very quickly she went away. In the meantime, while all this was going on, I hadn't a clue to what was happening. I heard from what seemed far away Pesach's voice yelling, "Where is she, where did she disappear to?"

Over and over he asked for me. For the longest time, I kept hearing his voice as he circled the outside of the Kowaliks' property. Eventually, I stopped hearing him. I didn't move a muscle. I lay there thinking that Mama had left me here with crazy Pesach. She wanted me dead. Jewish children were just garbage now. Oh, God, why was all this happening? What did we do wrong? The Jewish people never hurt anybody. The Jews, if anything, had always contributed so much good to the world. Just in my town, Goray, Jews were merchants, tailors, innkeepers, barbers, bakers, and candlestick makers. You name it, the Jews did it – they worked hard and supplied the farmers, as well as the others, with conveniences. Of course, they wanted to get paid for their work. But who doesn't? Jews were good, solid citizens. While thinking all kinds of thoughts, I fell asleep.

I must have been asleep for several hours when I was awakened by a sound. I opened my eyes, and it was dark – pitch black. It took me a moment to realize I wasn't in our original hiding place with my mother. I was alone. The sound soon became a familiar voice. It was Juzefka Kowalik quietly calling my name. But I didn't move. She pulled away the straw, and I could see her pretty face as she held up the lantern. "Here," she said, as she handed me my shoes and stockings. "Put them on and come. I have a good surprise for you in our house."

I was somewhat in a daze, but I walked with her, and somehow a pleasant feeling of hope began inside me. "Open the door," she said. I hesitated, so Juzefka opened it for me.

I walked into the kitchen, and several members of the Kowalik family were there. All of them were staring at me – except for one woman, whose head and part of her face were covered with a dark gray shawl. She turned toward me and said, "Naomi?" I couldn't believe my eyes – it was my sister Janice!

She took my hand and pulled me toward her. We hugged and cried and hugged some more. It was late at night. Looking at me as if she were reading my thoughts, she said to me, "Mama is with us in our hiding place. She was attacked by Mrs. Kowalik's dog, who bit her when she tried to go close to Mrs. Kowalki's house. She also decided that Mrs. Kowalik won't want to keep all of you, so she came to us. Tonight she sent me here to get you away from Pesach somehow and bring you to our hideout. So come, get under my shawl, and start walking. We have a long walk ahead of us."

"Wow!" I thought. "So Mama never did leave me for good! No, she didn't desert me. I'm still her baby."

The hiding place at Mrs. Sosnowich's was just the way Mama had described it to me after she found Janice and Josh – terrible! They pulled out some more hay in that cave and made it a little bigger so Mama and I would also fit in. But at least now we were all four together, plus Shlomo, the young man from Goray, who was there first. So we were five.

Every evening Zosha slid on her belly with a lantern tied to her and a pot of good mashed potatoes for us to eat. Some nights she even brought along some bread and cheese. My sister would open two boards and take the food from her. Sometimes Zosha would stay a few minutes, usually talking to Shlomo. We each would reach inside the pot in the dark and scoop out the mashed potatoes with our hand. Umm, delicious! But soon the pot would be empty, though my stomach wanted more. I'd tell myself that tomorrow there will be more. Every night Mama would let someone else scrape out the pot. When it was my turn, I literally put the pot over my head and licked out every speck of food. It kept me busy for a long time. But when I was through with the pot, it was clean.

As the saying goes, all good things must end. And so did our stay at Mrs. Sosnowich's. Our welcome there was wearing out, like Zosha's body from crawling under the floor of the barn. After six weeks, by the end of February 1943, Zosha came with the food and bad news.

"My mother says that this is the last meal you will get from her. Mother and I have pity on you, but we can't keep this up any longer," she said. "You will all have to leave right away. So you'd better be gone by morning."

My mother started begging and saying that Zosha didn't have to bring the food to us, that we would crawl to the yard and take it from her. Also, we didn't have to be fed every night – it could be every second night. But Zosha just left, saying, "No, no!"

Once again our hopes were diminishing. Soon after Zosha left, Shlomo declared that he was going right away. He said good-bye to us and was ready to take off.

"What is your hurry?" asked my mother. "Maybe she'll change her mind, maybe we can hide here and take turns getting some food somehow. And, Shlomo, you can be of help to us."

He replied that he knew the Sosnowiches, and if they said to leave, they meant it. He had to think of himself first. What we didn't know then was that Shlomo had promised to marry Zosha when the war was over. Zosha, it seems, was in love with Shlomo and had decided to hide him only.

Two days passed by with no food. We grew weaker. My mother said we had better crawl out of there while we were still able to and try some other way to cling to life.

For the next few days, we were back to the way Mama and I were after we escaped *Judenrein* in Frampol. We knocked on people's doors and windows, we begged for food and some kind of shelter, but the results were pretty much the same. Some villagers gave us bits of food and told us to leave. Others tried to take us into town to be killed by the Germans. Still others tried killing us themselves. But we still managed to escape.

One nice man, who said he was good friends with my grandfather on my mother's side, put us up in his attic for one night and gave us some food to eat. The next night he came up, drunk and with a rifle in his hands, yelling, "*Żydy*, get out of here right now or I'll kill you!" He chased us down quickly and shot in the air as we ran for our lives. One of his sons knocked my mother down to the ground – I saw him raise his hand, holding a knife to strike my mother, when his drunken father shot again in the air and shouted to his son, "Let them go! Let somebody else kill them!"

We continued to run very fast. When we realized that no one was chasing us any longer, we stopped running, caught our breath again, and began to just walk in the white snow. It was a clear night. I gazed up to heaven with a heavy heart. What now?

"Look," I heard Janice say. "Look at that huge *kopniak* [haystack] right in the middle of the field!"

"The village people prepare these haystacks for extra food for their animals in the spring," explained Mama.

"But, Mama, don't you see," said Janice, "we can dig a hole on the bottom and hide in there for now. It will keep us warm."

My mother said she'd had it by now with trying to hide and run. But we were already busy pulling out hay. The frozen hay came out in big chunks. As soon as we could all four fit in that hole on the bottom of the *kopniak*, we crawled in and curled up so as not to take up too much room. Josh and Janice pulled over most of the outside hay to close the opening. Exhausted, we fell asleep.

The next day we were all very hungry, suffering from the cold, and stiff from having no room to move. But we had to wait until nightfall to go out to look for food. We put out our hands to bring in some snow to lick on all day. In the evening Mama said that she and Janice would go out to try and get something to eat. Josh whispered in my ear, "You know they will never come back to us if we let them go by themselves. It's easier for grownups to find a place with gentiles. Kids are trouble now."

So I grabbed onto Mama, and Josh and I told Mama and Janice our feelings. "All right," said Mama. "If you feel this way, we won't go. But you are both wrong."

"Let's go. Don't listen to them," said Janice. "They are slowly dying, and so will we if we don't move right now. Let's go!"

For several hours Josh and I lay quietly without a word said. Then suddenly we could hear the crunching of their feet in the snow. In they came with bread, a container with some milk, and good news. My mother and sister had to soak the bread in the milk and help Josh and me open our mouths. They ordered us to try to chew. We were very weak by now. "Crazy kids," said Janice. "They almost died!"

But soon we were feeling better, and we asked about the good news. Janice did most of the talking. "We walked out of here and walked for about a mile, when we saw a house in the distance. Sure enough, it was the first house of this village, and you know who lives in the first house of Lada? Yes, the Kowaliks! Mother and I went in and, of course, Mrs. Kowalik crossed herself and yelled out, 'Jesus Christus, you always scare me!'

"But this time she was a lot nicer to us. Mama told her all about our bad luck and asked if she could find it in her heart to take pity on us and hide us somewhere on her property. Mama assured her that we need very little food to get by. 'And God will reward you with long life, and many other good things will come your way,' Mama told her. 'I will go to see Mr. Zlomainsky. I'm sure he will help your family with some money and maybe some other valuables.'

"She listened very closely to Mama, and then she told us that last Sunday she had seen Mr. Zlomainsky in church. He told her that the war might end soon and that if she found us, the Rosenbergs, she should put us up. He also told her that he would pay her to keep us. She believes in Zlomainsky. She says he's smart.

"'So, I'll take you and your children in,' she said. 'I will hide you under the floor of my barns. It's damp and cold there, but if Saverek Zlomainsky is right, who knows? You may even survive the war.' Mama got on her knees and kissed her hands, and so did I," said Janice.

Hope. "There is hope once again!" I thought. Josh and I perked up quickly. We finished the bread and milk. "All right," said Mama. "Let's get out of here!"

We crawled out of the *kopniak*. It was snowing now. All I could see were open fields covered with snow. The wind was in our faces, and it was hard to walk. But my mother said that it was good, because the fresh snow would cover up our footprints. As we got close to the Kowalik property, we could see Maria Kowalik walking toward us. "Come this way," she said.

She pointed to her barns and stables, which were downhill from her house, about three hundred yards away. She unlocked a huge door and opened it. We entered the courtyard. Her barns and stables were built in a sort of square, with a courtyard inside. To the right was a whole row of stables. First the pig stables, then the horses and ponies. The last several stables had many cows. To our extreme left was a whole row of barns filled with hay on the upper level and grain on the lower level. That was feed for the animals in winter and early spring. Straight ahead from us, but to the right, was an exit or entrance for the animals to go out in the summer and graze in the field. The two huge wooden gates also served as an exit or entrance for horse-drawn wagons. These wagons were stored on the left side of the gates, against the wall. Above these huge walls were lofts or attics filled tightly with hay and straw. At the very end of this wall, to the left, was a small end barn packed inside from floor to ceiling with hay. There were also barns with chicken coops, geese, and ducks. Mrs. Kowalik walked us over to the small end barn next to the wagons, where she stopped and started talking.

"You see, all my animals are branded. They are confiscated by the Germans. That means we can't kill any of our cows or pigs and eat meat. So when a sow has a litter of piglets, I hide them down here," she said, as she pulled out some long nails and took down the boards. "It's a good hiding place," she told us. "Tonight, I removed the piglets from here and put them some other place after I saw you. Now you Jews can have their *kriuvka* [hideout]." She put down her kerosene lantern on the ground and looked at us very closely. "I hope I'm doing the right thing," she said.

She then picked up the lantern, and we could see a hole made inside the straw. Mrs. Kowalik stepped up to that opening hole and said to us, "Follow me." She wiggled from side to side like a snake, going downward with the lantern in front so she could see. We each followed her down the straw path until we hit the ground. "Now you are inside the foundation under the first floor of the barns. Crawl with me, bearing right on the ground, and I'll take you to the highest part of the foundation," she said.

After awhile, she stopped. She put down the lantern and sat down sideways, leaning a bit back. She pointed to the straw bed on the ground. There was a bad odor all around us, left from the piglets, I guess. But we all ignored it and listened to Mrs. Kowalik. "I cleaned up as best as I could tonight after I removed the piglets, and I put fresh straw on top. Here is a burlap sheet to cover yourselves. I know it's cold here. So get close to one another and you'll feel warmer. Tomorrow I will bring you some food."

Then she started crawling away. She turned back somewhat and said again, "God only knows if I'm doing the right thing, risking my whole family because of Jews." Now she was leaving, and my mother crawled after her, thanking her and telling her that the Almighty would reward her for saving human lives. And that next Sunday, when she would see Mr. Zlomainsky in church, to tell him about us. "Yes," Mrs. Kowalik answered.

Before exiting into that short tunnel, she warned us, "Not a sound out of you while you are here. The walls have ears. You never know who can hear you and give you out to the sheriff. If you have to talk, do so in a whisper. I know you have toilet needs. We will talk about that tomorrow." She left with her lantern, closed the two boards, and we were left in complete darkness.

When dawn came, I awoke hearing noises from the animals as well as from people. The Kowaliks were doing their morning chores, feeding all the animals, milking the cows, and grooming the horses as well as feeding grain to the chickens. I was curled up between my mother and my sister. Josh was lying down on the other side of Janice. It was very cold. I tried not to move, remembering Mrs. Kowalik telling us to be silent. I was hungry. We all thought, "Soon, soon she will bring us food." But she didn't come until it was night.

Inside the *kriuvka*, it was dark. The only bit of light came from the little cracks in the foundation wall, which was made of stone sealed together with lime and sand. Looking at my family that first morning was scary. All I could see was someone's eye, or hand, or nose when the bit of light was on them. I was able to sit down without my head touching the first floor above us. So could Josh. But Mama and Janice, being taller, had to sit with their heads bent down toward their chests or lean to the side. It was a huge crawl space, and bits of light came through all over the foundation. After awhile, it seemed to get lighter inside. Hungry, thirsty, cold – but most of all, scared – we passed the first day in our hiding place lying down very close to each other.

When night fell, Mrs. Kowalik knocked on the boards and called for my mother to come up and get the food. She didn't want to call my mother by her name, Faiga, because it was too Jewish, so she decided to call her "Stara," which in Polish means "Old Woman." (My mother was only thirty-nine years old!) Mama hurried to the passageway, and since she still had a normal, not-too-skinny build at that time, she had some difficulty climbing up and coming down. But she returned with a pot full of potatoes boiled in the skin. Mama gave out the potatoes in the dark by whispering our names. We each got three potatoes that were still warm. On the bottom of the pot was a little water with dirt from the potato skins. We each took about two sips and passed the pot on to the next person. By the time it got to me the water was gritty, but I knew I must not complain.

We all ate without uttering a word. Then Mama told us that we would have to have to get used to the once-a-day potatoes because Mrs. Kowalik had told her that that was all she could bring us. She said that she had to pretend she was taking these potatoes to her young animals. Too much activity could cause suspicion among outsiders, she said. Her seven children all knew about us. But her son-in-law Chaika, who was married to her oldest daughter, Wlatka, hadn't been told. "He wouldn't stand for Jews being hidden on our property, and since he and Wlatka live in my house, it's better not to tell him," said Maria Kowalik.

After about a week in the kriuvka, Mama asked me to be the one to get the food from the Kowaliks. She thought that since I was small, it would be easier for me to climb up and down the small tunnel with the pot of food. I liked having that job. I would hear the familiar knock and crawl on all fours very fast to get the food. By now we had a wooden bar inside and a slide on each side of the two boards that would open. Most of the time I just opened one board. I learned to unlock, get the food, and lock up again very quickly. Now the boards on the outside would not open. It felt more secure this way. My sister would wait for me as I slid down this passage, and she would take the pot from me.

After doing my job for about a week, one night as I was taking the pot from Mrs. Kowalik, she lifted up her lantern. Staring straight at me with her gray eyes, she said, "My, you are wearing such a pretty dress." I looked down and realized that my coat was unbuttoned and my dress was visible. "Let me see it," she said. At first I was happy that she was admiring my pretty dress. But then she said to me, "You don't need such a pretty dress, hiding out in the ground. My Marinka, who is about your age, can enjoy the dress to wear to church."

I got cold all over. I started remembering the day my parents came home from a trip to Zamoshch. My mother was smiling, telling me that she had bought material for a new dress for me. What excitement! I, little Naomi, was getting a new dress, made especially for me! No, not a hand-me-down from my three older sisters or any girl cousins!

"Let's go to Rochel Leah, the seamstress, to have you measured for this dress," said Mama.

Oh boy, I'm almost eight years old, and I'm getting a dress made especially for me! How do you like that? "I'll show the people in this town who has a new dress," I thought to myself. "Yes, me! I, chubby little Naomi, am going to have the nicest, the most beautiful new dress, made especially for me! Nobody has worn this dress before me, nobody gets measured and fitted for this dress but me. This dress is not worn out with *latas* (patches) in places. It's new!" The material felt so soft and clean. It even smelled terrific! "When I walk out in this pink polka-dotted new dress, every person will stop and stare and admire me in my new dress."

Days and weeks passed before Rochel Leah found time to finish my first and only new dress. On the holiday of *Shavuot*, I put it on for the first time. I looked in the mirror, and I liked what I saw. It had puffy sleeves and lots of material around the waist. It was roomy so that I could grow into it and wear it for a long time. I twirled and twirled, round and around. I would look in the mirror and see the skirt of the dress looking like a full circle. I was so happy! I loved my new dress.

Now Maria Kowalik says to take it off and give it to Marinka? "No!" my insides screamed. But I knew our situation, and I knew Mama would want me to give it to her. So I took it off and handed it to "long-face" Kowalik. I put my coat back on, buttoned it, and closed the wall inside.

The next day Mrs. Kowalik brought me a used boy's shirt, made of an ugly gray material. That material was very strong, because I wore this shirt for about a year and a half, never taking it off.

If thoughts could write instead of the hand and eyes, I would probably have many volumes written already. So very often I think of my past and of the many interesting things I witnessed in my young life. Most things I remember were difficult to live with. They were sad. But I also remember things that were good, even humorous. True, not everyone appreciates the same kind of humor. So what? Right now everything is jumbled in my head. I have no idea what I really want to tell you, except that I'm in a talkative mood. So bear with me.

During World War II when we, the Jews, became the scapegoats, Nazi Germany occupied Poland with orders to wipe out its three and a half million Jews, to make Judenrein, so there would be no one left to tell of the suffering inflicted on us and what we witnessed. The horrors and inhumane behavior toward us were to be erased from future history. But I did survive, and I'm here today feeling an obligation at times to tell what I personally experienced and saw other people experience.

Let me see. People, and how they think, have always fascinated me – why they do certain things at certain times; why people from the same environment, with the same religious beliefs, and from the same geographical place can react quite differently. Two gentiles from my hometown of Goray in Poland come to my mind. One was Saverek Zlomainsky, and the other one was Stefan Mrożyk. Zlomainsky and Mrożyk were such complete opposites. I would like to tell you what I remember about these two men.

In Goray, Zlomainsky was considered a rich man. He had a leather factory. In early 1939 he would have been about forty-eight years old. He was married and had one son and one daughter. He was liked and respected by the gentiles as well as by the Jews. I remember him smiling often, shaking hands with people, tipping his hat while greeting ladies. He would rub the hair on my head when visiting our house and call me *kudlata blondinka* (curly blonde). "When you grow up," he would say, "You'll be a pretty young lady." Then he would ask me for a glass of water to drink, and I would watch him gulp it down while looking at me with his blue eyes. I used to think he was very handsome. His mustache was thick and well groomed. He was always well dressed.

I liked to listen to him conversing with my father. My dad and Zlomainsky were good friends. During the war they would always talk politics. At the beginning of the war, I was bored when they talked politics, so I used to run outside to play with my gang of friends. Of course, at age six I didn't understand much of their political talks. I just knew that bad things were about to happen, and I hoped it would get better very soon. There was a feeling that Zlomainsky was a good friend to the Jews, so they trusted him with some of their belongings to hide on his premises. Those Jews who had jewelry, fur coats, and silver items, as well as money, knew that when the war finally ended, Zlomainsky would gladly return these things to them. So when the SS used to come and demand the *reichtung*, people would give them just what was on hand.

"This, my friend, will be a bloody and costly war," I heard him say one day to my father.

To this my father replied, "But Hitler and his people will eventually pay dearly for it." And they both nodded their heads in agreement.

Occasionally, the priest from the big church in Goray would also be in our house and would join in their conversation. I remember him also as a pleasant person. As long as Jews and gentiles were still allowed to visit each other, these two nice men were frequent visitors in our house.

Stefan Mrożyk, on the other hand, was in his early twenties when the war broke out. He came from a very poor home. His family lived in a village several miles from Goray. He supported himself by working mainly for Jewish people. He would do all kinds of odd jobs in order to get paid. The Jewish merchants would call on him to work for them. He was always polite and managed to make a living. I remember him cleaning the shelves in back of my father's store and arranging the boxes that contained men's hats for sale. He also brushed and put the fur collars and other fur pieces in the proper places in the store. My father always praised his ability to do things. Daddy would pay him at the end of his work and bid him a good day. He was always thankful and asked for more work. My father called on him as often as he needed a helper. He also washed walls inside our house and mopped the wooden floor in our kitchen. He always seemed hungry when working in our house. So he would compliment my mother on the aroma of her cooking. She made sure he got a bowl of food, which he would eat heartily. Mrożyk always said thank you very politely to my mother, bowing his head as he would leave our house.

Mrożyk worked in many Jewish homes, and that was the way he supported himself. No one thought much about him. He was good-looking and polite, but the gentiles of Goray somehow disliked him. They forbade their daughters to speak to him or even be seen with him. He didn't attend church very often, and the townspeople thought there was something shifty about him.

When Nazi Germany occupied Poland in September 1939, the Jewish troubles began to develop. In 1940 Jews were confined to the area where they lived. It became known as the "ghetto" area. No Jews were allowed outside the ghetto to have any contact with non-Jews. Jews were told to give up their valuable belongings. Jews over the age of twelve had to wear an armband with the star of David on it and had to report every morning to the town center to be picked for *zwanks arbeit* (forced labor). As time went on, things got worse. More hard labor for more people, less food and water. Then the bread rationing started. Hunger, thirst, and living in unsanitary conditions became a daily struggle. Then came the slow process of killing the old people and the children. If you were either old or a child in those days, you were constantly worried that maybe tomorrow there would be an *akzia*, and they would catch you and put you on the wagon. We all knew what was happening to these wagons full of children and their grandparents. They were buried in the trenches that the strong adult Jews were forced to dig during so-called *zwanks arbeit*.

Ironically, the Germans couldn't accomplish all this on their own, simply because they couldn't always identify a Jew. Since we, the Jewish people, don't really have horns, many of us could have passed for non-Jews. But Hitler had no problem with that because many Polish gentiles happily volunteered to help the Nazis with their task. They helped round up the old men and women and the frightened children, and they whipped them if they resisted. Yes, the Polish gentile was of great help to the Germans! After all, the Germans were only temporary visitors in Poland, how could they tell us apart? But our so-called friends and neighbors knew each and every one of us Jews. This was a great time for the anti-Semites. To humiliate the Jews was a good deed. To beat an old man or woman, or to take a young child from a mother's arms and watch that mother and father try to fight them, was a special sport enjoyed by many non-Jews. And that's when our polite Stefan Mrożyk had himself a field day.

When the Gestapo and the SS came to Goray, Mrożyk came to greet them and announced that he and his buddies were willing to do whatever the Germans asked of them. Mrożyk declared himself a Nazi, and he was sworn in as a full-fledged party member. The people of Goray were in shock. It was bad enough to have the Germans to worry about. Now they also had Mrożyk to help them. And, my God, how he helped them!

One afternoon in 1941, Mrożyk, with some of his gang, came bursting into our house and told my father, "Pinchas Rosenberg, you are under arrest!"

"Why, Stefan? What did I do wrong to be arrested?" asked my dad.

My mother tried to push Mrożyk away, so he pushed her very hard, and she fell against the wall. Without replying to my father, they handcuffed him and put him in jail. The same day they also arrested five other Jewish men in town. We all cried, fearing that Mrożyk would kill our Daddy. The next day my mother received a note delivered from Mrożyk, telling her to bring to him a large sum of money if she wanted her husband back alive. My mother was trembling as she read Mrożyk's note to herself. She sent us children to bed that night, but she must have been up all night discussing things with my oldest two sisters, Chaya-Leeba and Perele. I could hear whispering, and I could also see the kerosene lamp in the kitchen burning all night.

The following morning, Mama went to Mrożyk to deliver the money he demanded. Then she kept looking out the window from behind the curtains all afternoon, hoping to see my daddy come home. Daddy came home when it was already dark. We all hugged him, but his face was sad. He didn't say anything for quite some time. Then he told us how Mrożyk had killed four of the men, and only he and Moishe Binom were left. When Mrożyk unlocked the jail door for him and Moishe, he thought they were going to their death. He later said that he was glad to be alive and at home but that he was very sad for those who were killed by Mrożyk. "Mrożyk, like Hitler and his people, will eventually be punished for all the horrors he is causing now, but I can only hope that we will as a family all be here to see that day," my father said.

Mrożyk terrorized our town. People feared him as much as they feared the SS and the Gestapo – some days even more. Beating up a Jew gave him pleasure. Humiliating Jews was fun for him. He would make some Orthodox Jews chew and swallow bacon only because he knew it was against the Jewish law to do so. He asked the town's rabbi to sing Christmas carols, and when the rabbi explained to him that he didn't even know any Christmas songs, he whipped him mercilessly with his rubber hose so that all his buddies would see and laugh.

In the early days of the war, I remember my zaida, Aaron Yankel (Mama's father), knocked on our door one evening. When Josh and I saw him, we burst out laughing. My mother came running over and said, "This is not funny!"

Mrożyk had somebody enter our synagogue with him, and this time they picked on my zaida. They shaved his head, eyebrow, and beard on the right side only. Zaida Aaron Yankel had bushy eyebrows and thick brown hair and beard. There was some blood running down his face. To Josh and me, our zaida looked funny at first. But when we heard him tell us how humiliated he felt, we were really sorry for having laughed.

When the Germans wanted to know which Jews had money or other valuable things, Mrożyk gave them a list of names. Mrożyk appointed young, strong Jewish men in their early twenties to be policemen. They were told that if they didn't obey his orders, or the orders of the Germans, they would be shot to death. When the first official *akzia* occurred in Goray, the Germans ordered one hundred

Jewish children and old people to be rounded up. They were taken out of town, killed by the Germans, and buried in a mass grave. We all knew about it because they made no secret of it by now. Mrożyk, of course, came to assist the Germans. He ordered the Jewish police to round up the poor souls about to be killed. They were put on horse-drawn wagons, never to be seen again.

After that first *akzia*, Mrożyk found out that four of the Jewish policemen had refused to send children and old people to their deaths. The next day he and his gang rounded up these four heroes. Their hands cuffed behind them, they were marched through town for all to see. We Jews were all inside looking through sheer curtains as the SS and Mrożyk marched by our houses with our four men who wouldn't send innocent people to their deaths. We stood paralyzed in great distress when we heard the shots, one after another.

Several hours had passed by when we heard an announcement through a loudspeaker: "*Żydy!* You may now see your good but dead policemen and bid them goodbye by burying them." Etched in my memory is a picture of the four once-lively friends, lying still. Three of them faced down. One was on his back, his eyes open as if he were about to say something – but he couldn't. I looked at his blue eyes and golden-red hair. There were many people who came to see them in silence. Soon their parents came. Their mothers, sobbing, held their sons in their arms for the last time. And so it went. Another funeral, and Goray buried four more of its brave.

Not a day went by now without bad, disturbing, and humiliating things happening to us, the Jews of Goray. More and more arrests were made by Mrożyk and his gang. More killings of Jewish men, if their families couldn't satisfy his demands for money and other valuable things. My father was arrested by Mrożyk countless times. This tyrant must have been very observant when he worked for the Jews before the war. He would demand not only money from my mother, but also her jewelry - the diamond brooch given to her by my father as a gift on a special occasion; her antique gold chain, an engagement gift from my dad; the three strands of cultured pearls that she used to wear on her long, beautiful neck on holidays; and her gold and diamond rings. All that, plus whatever else he knew that Mama had, he would now demand. And to keep on saving my father from Mrożyk's bullets, Mama would hand him these things. Every time he released Daddy from jail, six or eight other Jews would be killed by these murderers.

I remember Daddy came home one evening, sad as usual. Mrożyk had killed eight other men. Their families would be allowed to bury them the next morning. That evening after dark, Mr. Duvid Weinschtein, the tailor, realized sometime after the shooting that he was not dead. He was alive and could move. He was shot in the shoulder and on the face near his ear. He freed himself from the dead bodies lying on the ground, and he made it home to his family. Knowing Mrożyk, his family decided to put him in their hiding place under the floor.

The next day when the madman Mrożyk found out that Mr. Weinschtein was alive, he came marching into his house and demanded, "Where is he?" When the family fearfully denied knowing anything about him, he shouted, "Jews are always lying to me!" He then shoved their dining table aside, yanked the rug off the floor, and opened the trapdoor to their hiding place. He cold-bloodedly shot several bullets into Mr. Weinschtein and stormed out of the house. (To talk about Stefan Mrożyk is still very disturbing to me, but I feel I have to. At this point in my life, I must tell. For if not now, when?)

Once Mrożyk had his fill of Jewish money and jewels, he would then demand young Jewish girls and would rape them in exchange for their fathers' temporarily spared lives. At nine years of age, I didn't understand rape. But I will never forget the last time he arrested my father and asked for my oldest sister, Chaya-Leeba, to come see him. I saw her crying bitter tears. My mother kept moving nervously. I asked Mama, "Why can't Chaya-Leeba go to see Mrożyk, if that will make him release Daddy from jail?"

Mama yelled at me for asking things she couldn't explain to me. She said I made her more nervous and that I should stay out of her way. "Stay in the other room!" she ordered.

While in the next room, I was quite upset but also curious. So I listened from behind the door and heard Mama talking to Chaya-Leeba. "You will have to go to him," she said. "But I have a plan. I hope to God it will work. Do you hear me, Chaya-Leeba?"

Chaya-Leeba asked in despair, "What kind of plan can you come up with? My life is at an end. It's over!"

"No," said Mama. "Listen, child, I'll go to the slaughterhouse with rags and bring them home for you dipped in blood and smeared with ashes to put inside your underwear. You will be so dirty, he won't even touch you. I will also give you an envelope with a big sum of money inside. He doesn't realize I still have cash put away for life-threatening times like now."

I heard all this, but for the life of me, I didn't understand. The only thing that I understood was that things were terrifying. That evening I walked into the bedroom, and there was Chaya-Leeba, staring out the window and looking very sad. I knew that the shutters were closed and that my oldest sister couldn't see out like she was pretending to. I walked over to her. She was nineteen years old, so beautiful and so sad. (People used to say that I resembled her. That made me happy because I always wanted to be like her.) I went very close to her and looked up into her face. She put her arms around me, drew me close to her, and held me tight. I felt her tears dripping down on my head. The next morning when I walked into the kitchen, I found Mama, Perele, and Janice sitting on the floor and praying to God. They were saying *Tehillim* (Psalms). Chaya-Leeba was not at home anymore. Our house was a very sad house that day – more than ever before. That afternoon, my father came home with Chaya-Leeba by his side.

Life in the ghetto worsened. Now, in 1942, people were dying from hunger. Diseases were thriving in the unsanitary conditions. Practically everything was taken away from the Jewish people. The stores owned by Jews were now confiscated. I remember that the Germans put red-hot wax on the doors of my father's store, then put their stamp on the wax. "If the stamp is found broken, it will be punishable by death!" they shouted.

Everything was now punishable by death. No business transactions were allowed between gentiles and Jews. Shoemakers were not allowed to make shoes; dressmakers could no longer make a dress for a girl or woman if she wasn't Jewish. All Jewish merchants were out of business, and many had already been dispersed to other towns. The *akzias* continued more frequently. Life was difficult. There was nothing now but despair.

In late August of 1942, I believe, the last *akzia* before *Judenrein* occurred in Goray. Josh and I were hiding in our double-walled attic hideout with our maternal grandparents. They were rounding up Jewish children and old people. My bubbie Shaindel and zaida Aaron Yankel were sitting on the floor. Josh and I would look outside through the cracks between the wallboards. We saw Germans hitting Jews, telling them to go line up. We saw our former gentile neighbors delivering Jewish children to the Germans to be killed outside of town.

On this day I remember looking out and suddenly recognizing

the two little boys being carried upside-down by an SS man. He carried them by their feet in one hand, and in his other hand he carried a hatchet. The crying children – Mechal, five, and Usher, three – were my little cousins. They were my mother's only sister Hudel's precious sons. I turned around quickly toward my grandparents. My heart was beating rapidly. For a minute or so, I don't recall hearing or seeing anything at all. Then I saw my bubbie Shaindel, her elbows on her knees and her hands over her face. She was crying. I heard her say, "The innocent children are crying with such fear in their voices, because they feel they are going to die. Hear them, O Lord! Don't forsake them!"

My poor grandmother didn't know that those frightened cries were coming from her two gorgeous and loving grandsons, Mechal and Usher. My brother Josh, I saw, was lying on the floor, curled up facing the other side. I've never asked him what he saw that day. It was always a very painful subject to discuss. Yes, bullets were now too good for some Jewish children, so Usher and Mechal were hacked to death.

In September of 1942, the day after Rosh Hashanah, the Jewish new year, a big fire started in Goray. In a very short time smoke and the flames raged out of control. My parents ordered us children not to waste time but to grab whatever we could and quickly get out of the house. I put on my new polka-dotted dress, grabbed a pillow, and ran.

We gathered on the tall grass in the meadow behind the big church of Goray. As we stood there and watched our hometown burning, I saw many people with the belongings they had managed to save before the fire got close to them. The heat from the flames and the September sun made it extremely hot, even though we were quite a distance away from the actual fire. Everyone was seeking a bit of shade under a tree, but few of us could find it. People were worried about their fate. What would happen to us Jews? Would the Germans deport us to another town? Would they let us live together with the people whose properties didn't burn to ashes? We all knew that now we were in great danger.

A rumor was circulating that the Germans would gun us down with machine guns, with the help of many Polish gentile collaborators, until Goray was completely *Judenrein*. People were nervous to say the least. As the flames started dying down in the late afternoon, we learned that about a third of Goray had burned to the ground. My two sets of grandparents; my aunts, uncles, and cousins; and my friends and their families were all wandering around thinking what to do next. My uncle Moishe, Daddy's sister Chana's husband, came over from the other end of town. He told us that Mrożyk had accused a seventeen-year-old Jewish boy of starting the fire. Mrożyk had had him tied up with rope and thrown into the flames. "Poor boy," Uncle Moishe said. "He was burned alive."

Uncle Moishe said that there were rumors that the Germans intended to send all of us to *arbeits lagers* (labor camps) to which Jews were sent, but from which they never returned alive. The adults seemed to know about the concentration camps, because once in awhile someone would escape and tell what he had seen in these camps. Now, as the tension was building at the end of this hot September day, we heard a voice on the loudspeaker in Polish, then another voice in German. Mrożyk and several SS men, riding around town in a jeep, had decided the fate of the Jews of Goray. First we heard Stefan Mrożyk: "Attention all Jews! You must all report now to the marketplace, where you will all be put on trucks and wagons to take you to the nearest trains. The trains will take you to the *arbeits lager*, Majdanek, where you will work and live freely. Take all the belongings you have saved with you. No Jew is allowed in town anymore, except the marketplace. Jews who disobey these orders will be shot to death!"

Then an SS man's voice came over the loudspeakers. He started by saying, "*Achtung, achtung alle Juden!*" [Attention, attention, all Jews]. Then he more or less repeated the same speech that Mrożyk gave us. Shivers went through me – I really hated Mrożyk so much! When he said "Attention, *Żydy!*" I felt like digging my nails into his face, making him bleed the way he had made so many of us bleed. "Someday I hope to see him hang dead from a thick rope," I told myself, not really believing it would ever happen. Almost immediately Polish men went around next to the armed German soldiers, pointing out who was Jewish in case they had a problem identifying us.

"We must not give in," said my father. "Come, Faiga, and come, children, let us try to escape to my brother Shimon's house in Chshanov Lubelsky. That village is still livable for Jews." Chshanov Lubelsky was about fifteen or twenty miles from Goray. In the midst of all the confusion, people were saying goodbye to each other, tears streaming down their faces, hugging one another. The general feeling was that we would never meet again now that Goray was becoming Judenrein.

People tried to escape to any place they could, just not to wind up in Majdanek – that death trap! I was crying loudly as I said goodbye to my friends. As I was hugging my friend Yochi, I felt a hand on my neck. When I looked up, it was a German soldier. His other hand was on Yochi's shoulder. "*Juden?*" he asked his Polish sidekick.

But before he had a chance to get his answer, I pushed his hand off my neck and said to him, shaking my head side to side, "I'm not Jewish! Let me go. Let me go!"

"So go home, kid," he said as he held on to Yochi and pushed me away. I turned around and saw my family in the distance. I pushed my way through all the other people who looked so pitiful and sad.

"Halt, *Jude!* Halt, *Jude!*" I kept hearing Germans shouting. I'm not sure whether any of these "halts" were for me, but I never turned around. I just kept on running and pushing my way through until I caught up with my family.

My mother was ready to devour me for having slowed down the rest of the family just so I could have my good-byes with my friends. But my father quickly picked me up and carried me with one arm, while with his other hand he carried a valise. I buried my face in Daddy's shoulder and sobbed quietly.

When we arrived at my uncle Shimon's house in Chshanov at daybreak, exhausted from our long journey on foot, Uncle Shimon, his wife, and their three young sons were glad to see us, and that felt good. But after we had eaten some food and caught our breath, our uncle told us that the Germans had given strict orders to the Jews of Chshanov not to harbor any Jews from other towns. If they found anybody breaking their law, it would be punishable by death. So my father suggested that the seven of us stay in his basement for awhile until we could think of another plan. Uncle Shimon agreed. He and his wife would bring us food and water whenever they could. It wasn't much, and we were all hungry. But as my father said, "A living Jew these days has to be hungry."

We struggled with our unsanitary accommodations and back-breaking sleeping conditions for three days and nights in Uncle Shimon's cellar. My father kept asking his brother Shimon to find out if there were any towns in the vicinity where *Judenrein* was not yet declared. Uncle Shimon found out that Turobin, about thirty miles away, was one such town; so he hired a Polish man and paid him to take us to Turobin. Again we said our good-byes to family –

knowing by now that we might never again see them – and rode off in a wagon toward Turobin. About ten miles from Turobin, the Polish man ordered us out of his wagon. He said that he was afraid to be caught helping Jews.

"No use discussing it any further," said my father. "Let's walk the rest of the way before dawn. It's somewhat safer at night."

In Turobin my father had a cousin whose name was Shulom. Daddy told us that his cousin had a big house and garden. When we arrived, the house was full of people from neighboring towns and some other countries like Czechoslovakia and Germany who had also been dispossessed. But my dad's cousin told my father not to worry. He would make room for us somewhere. The four of us sisters slept in the attic. He took my parents and my brother Josh into his and his wife's bedroom. We observed Yom Kippur, the Day of Atonement, in Turobin under very trying conditions. It was the last holiday that our immediate family were alive and together.

Two days after Yom Kippur there were announcements posted all over Turobin that said, "All Jews must report at the center of the Turobin Jewish Ghetto to be deported to *arbeits lagers*." After October 15, 1942, any Jew found in Turobin would be shot. Once again, the big shock of *Judenrein*.

"No more running. No more hiding," said my father. "Es iz 'arois a g'zairah' az alle Yidden darfen yetzt umkummen in Europeh. Mir kenen dos nisht enderen. Mer nisht loifen. Men darf shtarben, tzuzamen mit alle Yidden. Dos iz Gots gibaut." [A decree came to pass in Heaven, that all Jews have to be annihilated in Europe. There's nothing we can do, we can't run any more. We have to die. Together with all Jews. This is God's will.]

When my sister Janice, who was fifteen, heard Daddy's words, she became hysterical. "No, no!" she cried. "I don't want to die! Not together with all the Jews or by myself! I want to live! I want to live, Daddy!" And she stormed out of the house.

My mother grabbed a gray wool shawl and said to my father, "How can we let one child run somewhere alone and never know what happened to her? I'm going with her. I will write and send you a note from wherever we are. I have some money with me." (Polish boys were sometimes paid to deliver notes to families in other towns. If they were honest, you were lucky to receive the note.) Then Mama too ran out of the house.

My father was nodding his head that it was all right. He turned to Chaya-Leeba and said to her, "You are my oldest child. Go with them. They will need someone who can think more clearly in these times of peril. Go, Chaya-Leeba, go." And she went.

Now Perele, Josh, and I were with our father in Turobin. Every hour that went by, I knew we were an hour closer to death. The agony of dying very soon consumed me. I was being torn apart inside. Yet we had been taught not to be disrespectful to our father. Every day my father talked to us a little more about the *olam habah*, the hereafter. He told us how good it would be after the one bad moment when we met with death.

"But, Daddy, why now?" we three kept asking.

"I don't know, my dear children. All I know is that we, the Jews of Europe, must die now."

Three days went by, and a gentile boy, whom my mother had paid to deliver a note, brought it to us. Mother wrote that the three of them, Chaya-Leeba, Janice, and herself, were now in the town of Frampol, where Jews were still allowed to live. She urged my father to bring us children and come at once. All three of us looked at Daddy with hope that he really hadn't given up yet and that he would take Mother's advice and go to Frampol, where we'd be together again.

"We will try to get to Frampol," said my father. "It's going to be difficult to get out of Turobin now that the ghetto is surrounded by Germans and Polish guards, so don't build up your hopes too much. But even if we are lucky enough and we make it to Frampol, it won't last. Frampol will become *Judenrein*, and then where do we run to?

I was worried. We were all scared. But what scared me even more now was the way my father was talking so pessimistically. My dad was the world's biggest optimist. He always talked to us about the good in the world. He would point out the bright side and tell us that things always have a way of working themselves out for the best. "You have to have faith in the Almighty, and you have to have hope. Always have hope," my dad would say. But now he seemed so down, and no consoling words were heard from him.

But Daddy wasted no time in looking for a way to escape Turobin and get to Frampol. Several hours later he told us that he had a plan that he hoped would work. "Since we are densely surrounded by Germans and Polish collaborators, we must get out by water." Through water? What did that mean? We were nervously eager to hear Daddy's plan.

He told us he had hired a Polish man to take us in his rowboat across the water – the only place not guarded, for obvious reasons. The water was deep, and it was quite a distance to the opposite shore. "After we successfully cross over the water, we will walk toward Frampol," said my father. "Dress as warmly as you can, and take very little with you." At this point, we had very little to take anyhow.

As soon as it got dark, we started to walk to the body of water. I think it was a large lake. We had to sneak in and out of people's yards, then walk in a field for some time. Then we crossed a small forest and came to the meeting place. A man was waiting for us. He told us to get inside his rowboat.

The man sat in the boat facing us. He was a husky person

who didn't talk much. It felt eerie sitting in this little boat next to Daddy. Perele and Josh were sitting behind us. The water was very still. You could hear the oars hitting the water. The sound seemed loud. We were all silent. It seemed like a very long ride on the water.

When we reached land, we quickly got out of the boat. My father paid the man. They shook hands, and the man rowed away. The four of us started walking in the dark. First we walked through open fields. Then we entered a forest. We walked quietly for several hours in the woods. My father kept looking up at the sky. He told us that the moon and stars were his guides toward Frampol. I didn't understand it – but then, there were so many things I just couldn't comprehend. So I just kept quiet and continued to walk, feeling very tired and confused. I also felt depressed and fearful.

Suddenly, my father stopped. He stood still for a minute, then said that he wasn't sure any longer that we were on the right track toward Frampol. He suggested that since we were all tired, we should lie down and get a little rest. "After we rest a bit, I will be able to get my bearings and know which way we have to continue in the forest toward Frampol," he said.

We all welcomed the rest, and I must have fallen asleep immediately. I felt my father place his hand gently on my shoulder, trying to wake me. "Wake up, children," he said. "The sun will soon start to rise. I know now which way we have to continue toward Frampol."

"Oh, no! Not walking again," I thought. My feet hurt, and I just didn't feel like rising up and walking again. But walk we must.

"Yes," said Daddy. "We are walking in the right direction." He sounded a little more optimistic. "Let us walk close to each other. It's easy to lose one another in the forest," he said. He took my hand and held it firmly and reassuringly.

We had walked for only about half an hour when we began to see the end of the forest. "When we get out of this forest, we will cross this small village and continue straight on to Frampol," said my father.

I couldn't wait to see my mother again. I was hoping that Mama, Chaya-Leeba, and Janice would have some warm food for us and maybe a place with a pillow to put my head down. But my thoughts were just too good to be true. As soon as we came out of the woods, there stood a young Polish man, pointing a rifle straight at us!

My father knew this man and greeted him by saying, "Good morning, Stashek. It's me, your father's friend from Goray, Pinchas Rosenberg. And these are my children."

"It is no longer a good morning for you," Stashek said angrily. He was waving his rifle around and urging us to obey him or he'd shoot us. "I'm taking you in to the sheriff in the village. Come on, walk in front of me, straight on," he said.

"But Stashek, your father is the sheriff, and I'm sure he'll let us go," said my dad, reaching into his pocket. But Stashek hit his hand with the rifle. "I'm only trying to take some money from my pocket to give to you," said my father.

"I don't want your money!" he shouted. "Just do as I say!" And he made us walk in front of him with his rifle firmly in his hands, pointing at us.

We were all in shock – we just didn't expect to be caught now. With my father looking out for us, I was very hopeful we would make it to Frampol. As we were walking, rifle pointing at us, my father kept on saying, "You'll see, Stashek's father will let us go. We've been friends for a long time. Stashek, take the money and let us go."

My father turned around to face Stashek, but once again Stashek used his rifle to hit my dad and shouted, "Don't you hear me? I said I'm taking you in! I don't want your money, Rosenberg!"

So with tears streaming down my face, not knowing what was ahead of us, life or death, I held onto my father's hand and prayed to God to help us. As we got closer to the sheriff's premises, the horrible nightmare became real. There were many Germans in uniform with machine guns and all other kinds of guns and rifles in their hands.

"Oh, no, no, it can't be true! It's them! It's German murderers!" cried out Perele.

"Juden," yelled Stashek from behind us. The Germans raised up their weapons, pointing them straight at us.

"Halt Jude!" shouted one.

"Let's shoot them," I heard another voice say from among them.

Stunned, I told myself it was a nightmare from which I'd soon wake up. But soon enough reality set in, and I saw my life ending now at age nine and a half. I started screaming at the top of my lungs. I threw myself on the ground, clawing the dirt with my fingers and scratching with my hands while screaming on. I just didn't want to know exactly the moment when the bullets would penetrate my head and burn my brain. But in all my hysteria, I began hearing my father's voice begging the beasts to please let the children go. "They are so young and so innocent. Don't shoot them. Please let them go to their mother in Frampol."

So I also started begging. I wrapped my arms around one of these murderer's boots, and I begged and begged. "Lieber Herr," I cried. "Bitte Schenken sie mir das leben!" [Dear Sir, please spare me my life!] But he shook himself loose from me and kicked me in the chest several times, yelling all kinds of obscenities about Jews - how disgusting we were, and how they had to get rid of us. And as I was now flat on my back on the ground looking up at this murderer, he pointed his gun in my face, laughing and saying to me, "You will soon be dead, rat!"

In the background I heard the voices of Perele, Joshua, and my father, saying, "Shema Yisrael . . ." So I closed my eyes before dying, and I too praised the Lord, saying, "Shema Yisrael, Adonai Eloheinu, Adonai Echod" [Hear, O Israel, the Lord Our God, the Lord is One].

While the Germans around us were enjoying themselves, thinking they would soon have the pleasure of killing Jews, the sheriff convinced their leader to have us arrested for twenty-four hours, and in that time they could catch more Jews and kill us all at the same time tomorrow morning. So the laughing devil kicked me again and ordered me to stand up.

I didn't know why he wanted me to get up, so I refused. I wanted it to be over now. But hearing my father's voice saying the Shema, as painful as it sounded, was somewhat comforting to me, even as I was about to die, so I got up and ran over to him.

They locked us up in the sheriff's jail. I said to my father, "Why do we have to be in agony for another twenty-four hours? It would have been better to be dead by now!"

"No, child," said Daddy. "It wouldn't be better. Every minute of life is a gift from God," he answered me.

It was a one-room jail with bars on the small glassless window. There were several benches there without backs and several baskets filled with hay. This large room looked like a storage room. I looked at Josh and Perele now for the first time in what seemed eternity since we were caught. Josh was trembling. So was Perele. She kept saying, "Mama, Mama!"

My father seemed calm but sad. Now he was hugging Josh, trying to comfort his only son. It was rather dark inside this jail, but Josh's paleness was visible to me even in darkness. In times of danger, Josh found it hard to cry or make any sounds. He would just shake from fear. Perele would show her emotions by crying and talking to us.

After about an hour had gone by very quietly in jail, I asked my father whether he thought we would see a miracle happen and our lives spared. He said that God could make it happen, but we shouldn't build up our hopes. Instead, he wanted us to try to accept death, because that was what we would be faced with tomorrow. "It will only hurt for a minute, and then there will be heaven, *Gan Eden* [the Garden of Eden] for us forever," he said quietly.

He tried to tell us that everybody has to die. But we, it seemed, had to die now, so we must try to accept our fate. Just then we heard the iron bar being unlatched at the entrance. The door opened and the gang of Germans was standing behind the sheriff. There must have been eight or ten German officers and soldiers. My father went close to the opened door and again started begging those fierce-looking German murderers to let the children go to their mother in Frampol. I was standing close to my father now. He put his arm around me and continued to beg.

Among the harsh faces, I thought I saw a red-haired soldier in the back looking at me with tears in his eyes. I stared at him, then another German pushed in two more Jewish people, a man and a woman, caught trying to escape the way we had. The man was twenty-two-year-old Laibel from Goray, whom we knew, and the woman was twenty-year-old Malka from Turobin. The two of them just couldn't stop crying for the longest time. Being in the same situation, we knew how they felt, so we couldn't console them. But we cried with them.

After several more hours passed, no one was crying any longer. There was complete silence in jail. Only this horrible feeling inside me just wouldn't go away – this awful feeling that I would never again feel or hear or touch anything, that I would never again see my mother, and that she would never know what happened to me, her baby. These thoughts were literally making me claw the walls with my fingers. I visualized Mama crying, and that was even more painful. I turned to my father and asked if he thought Mama, Chaya-Leeba, and Janice would survive the war.

"I doubt it," he said. "The European Jews are being eradicated by the Germans and their helpers. Jewish life here as we know it is at an end," said Daddy. "Frampol may become *Judenrein* quite soon. Then what? Run to another town, only to find it becoming cleansed of Jews as soon as we reach there? No, my dear children, I really don't think that your mother and two sisters will outlive this war. And if by some unforeseen miracle they should survive," continued my dad, "they will be worse off than us."

"How can that be, Daddy?" I asked.

"For us, it will be over," said my father. "We won't feel pain any longer. But they will always miss us and hurt for all the loved ones they lost." Then he said, "Our family was like a shining menorah. We were seven beautiful lights when we were all together. Now, our shining menorah is breaking. The lights are burning out, and the menorah is falling apart." Tears were running down my dad's face as he spoke.

Then I heard more banging at the jail door as the iron bar was being lifted again. When the door opened, the sheriff's wife was holding a pot of milk and some slices of bread in her hands. The sheriff was by her side, and several Germans were directly in back of them. My father reached out with his hands, but not to take the food. He was begging once again, pleading for his children's lives. "Lieber Herr, bitte schoen, schenken sie die kinder das leben!" [Dear sir, please spare these children's lives!]

Once again he was pushed inside with a rifle, as Malka and

66

Perele took the food. During these few minutes when the door was open, I saw the same soldier standing behind the others, staring at me all the time. Then I clearly saw a teardrop falling from each of his eyes. The door was slammed once again and latched. I found myself thinking, as I was eating the bread, "Why was that red-headed soldier crying? He is a German, and Germans don't cry. They have nothing to cry about. They only give pain to others and cause the others to cry. Strange," I thought.

But I soon stopped thinking about that soldier, and the thought of our execution that would take place in the morning made the bread stick in my throat. Eating bread had no meaning any longer. So I put down the rest of the bread sadly, and while sitting on the floor, I put my head on my father's lap. From all the exhaustion of the day, I fell asleep.

I had a dream that Mindele, the pious woman from Goray, came to see us in jail. She said to me, "You will live, you will live!" And then she disappeared. I told the others of my dream.

But my father didn't want me to be hurting even more when they came to kill us in the morning, so he said to me, "Naomi, dear, it was a dream. Remember, it was only a dream, and Mindele, the pious woman, is dead and resting peacefully."

Morning arrived sooner than any of us wanted it to. We were dragged out of jail to be shot. The whole German gang with their ammunition were standing around, talking and laughing. We now felt like fish out of water – too scared to die, but too weak to fight any longer. As I lifted my eyes to pray to God, I noticed the redhead leaning against a tree and really crying, wiping his eyes with a handkerchief. "He seems to have pity on us," I thought. For a moment I felt a human touch inside me. "But what good is his pity, if that's what it really is, since they are about to murder us?"

But my father continued to beg for his children. He managed to get someone's attention and they were talking with him, I noticed. The sheriff was also in the crowd, talking to Dad. But a loud voice was heard from a grubby SS man, who yelled, "No, no, I will kill them all! All these Jews must be dead before I have my breakfast. So let us go!"

"No, sir." Another voice was heard. This time it was the red-headed soldier. "Sir, please, we have to talk," he said.

Then they all got together with the sheriff, and all we could hear was, "Yes!" "No!" "Yes!" "No!" Then everybody was quiet for about two or three minutes.

Finally the redhead came over to us. He bent down and said, "You children can go to your mother in Frampol."

"What about our father?" we all begged. "Please let him come with us to Frampol! Please!"

"What about us?" yelled Laibel and Malka.

The soldier looked deep into my eyes, then walked away. He returned with the sheriff after several minutes. They both sat down on the ground next to Perele, Josh, and me. This time the sheriff spoke to the three of us clearly in Polish. "You were all caught coming out of the forest," he said. "The Germans say that the adults might be Partisans, who attack Germans whenever they can. Therefore, they will take your father and the other two adults back to Turobin. If the Jewish Committee in Turobin agrees that they are honest people and not Partisans, they will go free and your father will join you in Frampol tomorrow or the next day."

We looked up at our father, and he had a painful smile on his face. "Isn't that good news?" he said.

We kids believed the Germans and the sheriff. We said goodbye to Daddy with a trembling hug, each of us. When he hugged me, he whispered, "It's today's miracle, Naomi."

The red-headed soldier and the sheriff walked with us to the sheriff's barn. There they helped us get on a wagon that had two horses in front and a man driving. The soldier got on the wagon with us and ordered the driver to start. The sheriff walked away, the driver hit the horses with his reins, and we started toward Frampol without Daddy. He would come tomorrow, we were assured. The red-headed soldier was facing us. Every time I looked up, I saw him staring at me.

"What are your names?" he asked. We each told him. "You know," he said at one point, "I have two children at home just like you two." He pointed at Josh and me. "They must be about your ages. How old are you?" he asked.

"I'm twelve," said Josh.

"I'm nine and a half," I answered.

"And I'm seventeen years old," said Perele.

He said his children were a boy and a girl, ages seven and nine. We didn't talk much longer after that.

We rode about two hours, then he asked the driver to stop. He told us to walk straight ahead and we'd reach Frampol in about forty-five minutes. He told us that he and the driver couldn't be seen riding into town with Jewish people. That would mean that they were helping Jewish children. We thanked him many times. We never saw the driver's face, but I have a feeling it was Stashek, the sheriff's son.

An hour later we reached Frampol. When we told Mother our story, she cried out, "Oh no, you stupid children, you left your father to die! We will never see him again! I'm sure they killed him! You believed the Germans?" Mama was pulling at her hair and crying.

"But, Mama, they said, . . . " I tried to explain.

But Mama, very hurt and very angry, said, "'They said' – and you crazy kids believed Germans and Polish sheriffs!"

I began to have that horrible feeling inside. What if Mama was right? No, she couldn't be!

That night my sister Janice gave me her pillow to lie down on. There were lots of people in the room, and everyone slept on the floor. We had a spot near the window. Before I fell asleep, I prayed to God that my daddy would come to us tomorrow or the next day. "Please, God," I prayed, "Show me that this one time the Germans were good to all of us and they weren't lying."

Two days went by, and my daddy didn't come. A man who escaped Turobin came to Frampol, and he came to see us. He told us that the sheriff had ridden into the Turobin cemetery the day before and delivered three corpses for the Jewish people to bury. One of these corpses was my father, Pinchas Rosenberg. This man and several other men had performed the mitzvah (good deed) of burying my father and the others.

The menorah had broken. Its crown had fallen off. The menorah shines no longer. We lost you, Daddy. Losing you at a tender young age was very painful, and the pain just never goes away.

Three weeks later, on November 2, 1942, many truckloads of German soldiers, armed with machine guns and wearing helmets, drove into Frampol and made the town Judenrein - cleansed of Jews.

___

In the early morning hours in our hiding place, we would always hear the familiar sounds of the animals starting to move around. The Kowalik family would come and do their morning chores. First they would clean the stables, changing the straw under the animals and putting down fresh bedding. Then they would feed all the animals. After that they would milk the cows, groom the horses, feed the chickens, and so forth. The clucking of the chickens, the mooing of the cows, and the sounds of the other animals would give me the feeling that a new day was here. Yesterday was over, and we'd made it to another day.

Since the activities in the stables and barns were noisy, I was less afraid to move a little, to turn around or sit up. In the morning, at least, I felt Mama wouldn't tell me not to make a sound because someone might hear me and drag us out to our deaths. She used to say to us that not only hoodlums but other so-called nice gentiles were constantly observing their neighbors and friends to see if they were harboring Jews. If they found out that they were, Mama said, they would drag these Jews to the village sheriff or to Goray and be rewarded with a bag of sugar. The Jews would be slaughtered by the Germans. Sometimes the villagers would kill the Jews themselves, just for pleasure, Mama told us.

Mrs. Kowalik would come with our potatoes in the evening, and quite often she would have horror stories about Jews caught and delivered to the Germans or Jewish women raped and killed by the village men. "Animals!" she would say. "These men are just bad animals!"

One night she came down carrying her lantern as usual. This time she told us about a woman from Goray who had come to her house with her seven-year-old daughter and her nine-year-old son. "They were starved, so I gave them some soup and bread to eat," said Mrs. Kowalik. "They fought over the food like animals. They were fighting and screaming so loudly that I asked them to leave," continued Mrs. Kowalik. "And the woman, Mrs. Lea T., asked if my sons would take her children to town to be killed."

Maria Kowalik told us that Mrs. Lea T. felt that her only possible chance to survive would be alone, without her noisy children, who fought with each other all the time. "'Nobody wants to take us in or help us in any way,' Mrs. T. said. I told Mrs. T. that my boys are

God-fearing people. They will have nothing to do with killing others - especially children!" Maria said angrily. Then she said, "I just threw them all out of my house, and I warned the mother of these unfortunate children never to come close to my property again."

Maria Kowalik looked at us kids, then at my mother for a long time before she backed up and crawled out from our *kriuvka*. I was trembling inside after having heard this story. My brother Josh pulled me over by my hair and whispered in my ear, "I told you, Naomi, no one wants Jewish children now." He continued, "We'd better do whatever Mama says to do without upsetting her more than she already is." He too was shaking with fear and cold.

Our hiding place was bitter cold and completely dark at night. At first when a rat would run by, we would all hold our breaths, thinking someone was coming to get us. But in time we realized that they were rats chasing mice.

The crawl space in this foundation was big. It was built under all of the Kowaliks' barns. But most of our ceiling was close to the ground. We occupied the highest point in the crawl space. At some places, even Josh and I couldn't crawl under.

Our toilet needs did remind us that we were humans. It seems that Mrs. Kowalik forgot about this, or maybe she didn't want to think about most of our human needs. So we had to think of what to do. Mama said we couldn't go out, even at night, and take a chance of being heard. Also four people, she said, would be too much traffic going in and out. But we all had the same needs. My sister Janice came up with the idea of crawling away from our nest and digging a hole in the ground for our bowel movements, covering them with dirt, and, at the same time, creating another hole for the next person. She also stressed the importance to all of us of holding in for one week. "After all," she said, "we eat only once a day, two or three boiled potatoes in their skin. That is not much food to hold in. And maybe that will keep us from being so hungry," she concluded. I trained myself to hold in even longer than a week. At first I thought it was a crazy idea, and I hated to go to the area designated as our toilet. I dreaded that I might dig up someone else's waste with my hands. But in time I realized it was the only solution to this problem.

As time went by even the rats stopped being scared of us, and they would march around during the day as well as at night. I would look at them and think how ugly they were with their long snouts and dirty tails. They reminded me of the drawings that the Germans posted on the walls of the post office and other buildings in our town for everyone to see. They even pasted these ugly posters in the Gemina (city hall) of Goray. Wherever one turned, there were drawings to be seen. I remember these posters very vividly. They showed a big rat with a dirty tail and a very long and dirty snout. The rat was facing the caricature of a Jew with a large head, beady eyes, a long nose, little feet, and no body. The feet coming out from under this long nose had dirt on them. The rodent's snout and the Jew's nose almost touched as they stared at each other. There were lice and other vermin crawling all over these two creatures. Underneath this drawing was written, "We will cleanse Europe of all Jews and all rats."

I used to stare at these drawings, horrified. I would hear the Jewish people read the words under these drawings. They were sad as they looked, and they cried as they walked away. The gentiles looked and smiled. The Germans - in their terrifying uniforms - and some Polish people laughed hilariously at the drawing of the ugly rat and the disgusting caricature of the Jew.

Now, in our hiding place, the rats and the Jews both fought for existence. We fought for the same kernel of wheat or barley that occasionally fell through the cracks of the floor above us. During harvest time the Kowaliks would bring the stalks of grain into the barn and beat them with wooden flails to separate the kernels. During this threshing, my brother Josh and I would crawl over and pick up the few kernels that fell to the ground through the cracks of the floor above us. We then brought them over to share with the others. We Jews, as well as the rats, were very hungry and were trying to survive.

By now we had a quilt-like burlap cover. Mrs. Kowalik had given Mama another gray sheet. Mama and Janice sewed the sheets together into a cover and stuffed it with hay. It itched all the time we were lying under it, but it kept us from freezing to death. The winters in Poland are very harsh; snow stays on the ground from November until April.

But worse than being cold, for us, was being hungry. One cannot really understand hunger pains unless one has experienced them. We all get hungry before eating a meal. We all fast for a day occasionally and get very hungry at the end of the day. So we think we have hunger pains. No. Those are not hunger pains. We know that at the end of the fast day, we have food in our homes to eat and drink to our heart's delight. Hunger pains are when you feel you want to bite the flesh of your sister, who is lying next to you, and suck her blood.

Oh, yes, I remember my hunger pains very vividly! I would crawl up our little tunnel and look through the cracks between the two boards that opened onto our *kriuvka* and watch the animals eat. I would keep swallowing air over and over until my belly ached. Oh, how I envied those animals! I remember one afternoon watching the Kowaliks bringing in bushels of rotten apples, apple cores, and potato skins and throwing all of them into the trough. Then they opened the stables and all the animals rushed over to the trough to feast on their goodies. My eyes nearly popped out watching them chew and drool over the food as they were eating. As I felt my tears and my saliva dripping onto my cold hands, I licked my hands without taking my eyes from those animals. "Lucky animals!" I thought. "Why couldn't I be one?" (Actually, I felt I *was* an animal in those days – an underprivileged animal.)

As I watched the animals eat, the Kowaliks went away to their warm house to eat their supper. And as the animals filled up, one by one, they returned to their stables. Now I saw nobody in the courtyard, nobody at the trough. But my heart told me there was still food inside it, even though I couldn't see it. So I quickly slid down and crawled very fast over to our nest, and with great excitement, I whispered to the others about this eating orgy by the pigs and cows that I had just witnessed.

"And if we hurry, since nobody is in the yard now," I said, panting in a whisper as my heart was beating rapidly, "before it gets too dark outside, we can get all the leftovers in the trough!"

Mama was quiet. She didn't say anything. To me that meant she didn't object. Janice and Josh both jumped up so fast that they banged their heads on our low ceiling. They quickly crawled after me, and we wasted no time opening and pushing the boards apart. In record time, we were at the trough, eating out of it, only with a much greater appetite than the pigs and cows had. We ate fast, all the while looking around us in fear.

"Let's not stay here too long," said Janice. "Someone might see us or hear us."

"Let's bring the rest of this food down to eat with Mama," said Josh. I lifted up my gray shirt, holding it with one hand to make a sack-like space, and used my other hand to put the potato peels, rotten apples, and apple cores inside my handmade pouch. Josh and Janice invented their own ways to store this food.

When we offered the food to Mama, however, she refused to eat.

She just kept saying, "You eat, you eat. I'm not as hungry as you children are."

We ate nonstop, trying not to think about what we were eating or how we were eating. After we finished all the food, we crawled under the hay-filled cover. I felt so full. So heavy. My stomach felt huge; I felt as though my stomach was hanging down to my knees. I tried to fall asleep, to not have to think about anything at all. But sleep didn't come. I started feeling nausea; then I started having this awful sickly feeling all over me. Janice and Josh were lying down still. Mama was lying down next to me, not making a sound. Only I was turning my head back and forth, back and forth. I turned one way toward Janice, then toward my mother. I felt disgusted.

All I could think of now was the ugly drawings of the Jew and the rat facing each other. There was the big-nosed Jew flashing before me, and then there was the dirty rat. One minute I felt I was that ugly Jew – all of me was this ugly, big, long nose. The next minute I felt I was the disgusting rat. Jew, rat. Jew, rat! I felt so miserable; I just couldn't stop turning my head. I hated myself. I wanted to scream. I tried to control myself, but my head just couldn't take it.

Suddenly, Mama put her hand on my head and face as I turned my head toward her, and she held my head down firmly as if to say, "Stop it!" Neither one of us said a word. As she continued holding my head down, I began to feel so sad, so unwanted and unloved by anyone in the whole world. I began to cry. Tears poured out of my eyes. I dared not make a sound, but I just couldn't control my tears. I sobbed like a small child, only without any noise. My mother's hand started to move. She stroked my hair, wiped my tears with her hand, and whispered, "Shhh, shhh, shhh."

I reached out with my hand to Mama and touched her neck.

I was afraid of her these days. She might tell me I wasn't behaving responsibly. She might say I was an unruly child. But Mama was not scolding me now. She was not lecturing me at all. She continued stroking my head. I moved my hand from Mama's neck down to her chest; a couple of snaps opened, and suddenly I found myself holding my mother's bare breast in my hand. I froze. I was sure Mama would bite my hand. After all, I was almost ten years old. Why was I holding Mama's breast like a small child being nursed by its mother? It had been many years since Mama had nursed me.

But Mama didn't bite. She didn't scold me. She didn't even seem to mind my behavior now. So I started to relax my hand, and Mama pulled me closer to her. A spark of love awakened in me. That spark of love came from my mother to me. "Yes," I thought, "Mama loves me."

So I lifted my head up and with it I found Mama's head. I pulled over even closer, and I whispered in Mama's ear, "Minnak."

Minnak had no meaning to anybody. I had never heard the word. I still don't know if it is a real word in any language. But at that memorable time, Minnak took on a really wonderful meaning for my mother and me forever. It means "Mama, I love you," and it means "Naomi, I love you." Just before I fell asleep, a thought entered my mind. Wouldn't it be really good if tomorrow the war would end, and we would be free to live forever?!

"I must go to see Mr. Zlomainsky," said my mother one day. "I have to make sure he continues to help us. This evening I'm going to walk to Goray to talk to him and see that he keeps rewarding Mrs. Kowalik. Maria hasn't threatened us as much or as often lately, and I'd like to keep it this way," continued Mama. "She is a good woman; she risks her life and her family's lives in hiding us here. Let's not forget that."

When it got dark, Mama left us to go see Mr. Zlomainsky. This time I wasn't left alone. I was with my older sister and brother. But I still got that awful feeling inside that Mama might not come back. "Let's pray to God for Mama's safe return," said Janice. We each prayed silently and waited nervously for Mama to come back.

Several hours passed, and Mama returned. She gave us the signal by knocking two times twice and two times once on the boards. Janice rushed up and opened the boards for Mama. Mama was excited about her visit to Saverek Zlomainsky. She told us that she had waited as usual in his storage room, hoping he'd come walking out of his house. This time his wife came out first, however. Mama called her over.

Mrs. Zlomainsky was startled when she saw Mama. She talked to Mama for a short time, then asked her not to come there too often. She was afraid that people in town might see her. She told Mama that many Jews came to them for help; they found it hard to turn any human being away. But with their only son being held as a prisoner of war in Germany and their only daughter married to a German officer, helping Jews didn't exactly fit into the picture. She then went inside and sent out her husband.

Mr. Zlomainsky told Mama the same things his wife had said, but she felt he was glad to see her. He told Mama that since Goray had become *Judenrein*, he had been helping over a hundred Jews who had escaped and were hiding out. But by now, six months later, about half of them had been caught and killed, or had frozen to death, or had died from starvation. He said he would like to see us survive and that we might stand a chance if we could hold out longer. The war, he said, had taken a more favorable turn for us. America was now at war with Germany, as was the Soviet Union. In his opinion, it wouldn't be over really soon, but Hitler would definitely lose.

He also told Mama that if Mrs. Kowalik could manage to keep us, he would help her quite generously. "Tell Maria Kowalik," said Mr. Zlomainsky, "that for the coming Easter holiday, I will put shoes on her and all her seven children's feet. I will give her material to make suits and dresses for her whole family, including her son-in-law, Chaika, who lives in her house but doesn't know that she's hiding Jews."

Mama seemed excited about the politics. She said that Zlomainsky was very intelligent and that he knew a lot. The Kowaliks only knew what the city people told them on Sundays in church. "I will tell Maria all that Zlomainsky told me today," said Mama. "And I'll lie a little by adding that he said that the war might end really soon. A little lie at a time like this in order to make her happy can't hurt," she continued.

Mama said that Mr. Zlomainsky asked her not to come again if possible. He told Mama he would see Maria Kowalik in church on Sundays and would deal with her directly. He was afraid the people in town were beginning to be suspicious about him helping Jews. Even though they respected him, they all knew what a good friend he was to the Jews. "Privately, they call me the Jewish Uncle," he had said. "The town is not the same since Goray became *Judenrein*," Zlomainsky told Mama. "I miss my Jewish friends. The others miss the Jewish merchants, tailors, and shoemakers, but I miss the people," he said sadly to Mama. "I hate the Germans and what they are doing to the world. It's unforgivable. I can't wait to live and see them get what's coming to them," he said.

It was nice to hear Mama talk and tell us all these hopeful things that she had heard from Mr. Zlomainsky. We all thought he was the greatest. The following Sunday, Maria Kowalik spoke to Saverek Zlomainsky in church. She told us she was pleased with their conversation.

In March of 1943, Mrs. Kowalik told us that another Jewish man would be coming to our *kriuvka* to hide out with us very soon. We were shocked to hear her say that. She told us that Srulki Citrinbaum, from Goray, had escaped and was in her house. She said that in the last two weeks he had almost died twice. Once he was nearly killed by the Germans, and when he arrived in her house about ten days ago, he was burning up with fever and collapsed on her kitchen floor.

Four days later, when Srulki came to our hiding place, he told us his story, which went like this: He and his sister Chancia had escaped from Frampol on November 2, 1942. They tried to hide in various places, but nobody wanted them. Eventually, the two of them found a group of Partisans in a dense forest. There they worked together as Partisans for several months. When the Partisan in charge of that area came to visit this group and found out that Srulki and Chancia were Jewish, he ordered the others to either kill them or take them into town to the Germans and collect the reward for bringing in two Jews.

Srulki was very sad as he was telling us his story. He said that while waiting for the Germans in Goray, they were locked up in a room with two Polish men watching them so they couldn't escape. He and Chancia begged and cried, trying to appeal to these two men to let them escape. But, he said, they had no consciences. They just whipped him and his sister and laughed at them. Srulki was twenty years old at that time, and his sister was eighteen. Srulki told Chancia quietly that they must try to escape. If they were lucky, they would make it. If not, they would at least die trying. So he smashed the window with his feet, he told us, and screamed to his sister, "Let's go!" But one man grabbed Chancia and the other one grabbed Srulki.

Srulki said he punched this man in the face with all the strength he had left and started to climb out the broken window. The man he punched grabbed Srulki by his arms as he was about to jump out the window. Srulki then slipped out of his jacket, which remained in the man's hands, and began to run for his life. The man holding Srulki's jacket jumped out the window and chased him. Srulki just kept running for the longest time without looking back, until he fell to the ground from exhaustion. He then realized that he had outrun the Polish guard. Soon he began to hear voices, and he realized that a whole gang of Polish boys was out now looking for him! He noticed a large rectangular box on somebody's property while he was lying on the ground. He went over, quickly opened the wooden box, and got inside it, closing the top. Farmers used these large wooden boxes to store flour in the summer to make bread. Now the box was empty. He curled up inside it and kept hearing voices saying, "Where can that Żyd be?"

They looked for him until it got dark. He told us he was so scared that he didn't leave the flour box for about a week. Srulki said he licked the walls of this box, which still had some dried-up flour stuck to them. He would also put his hand out at night and bring in snow to keep alive. After what he thought was one week, he began to feel very weak and sick. He thought he might die in this container, so one evening he managed to get out of it and began to walk. He said he was wheezing and coughing a lot. After walking awhile, he noticed a house on a hill in the distance and aimed toward this house. He said he wasn't sure whether it was really a house or whether he was hallucinating. When he entered the house, he collapsed. Juzefka helped her mother revive him, and she made him drink some milk. Maria Kowalik knew Srulki's family from Goray. His sister Rochel Leah, the seamstress, used to sew dresses for the Kowalik women. Srulki was a tailor.

Now Srulki needed help desperately. Maria Kowalik thought he was suffering from pneumonia as well as exhaustion, and she decided to help him get well. She put him in back of her wood-burning oven, where it was very warm. There she had a straw mattress and several blankets. She nourished him with food and lots of warm drinks.

Since the Kowaliks' house was the first house of the village and on top of a hill, Mrs. Kowalik would have many people visiting her. Mrs. Kowalik instructed her two youngest children, nine-year-old Marinka and seven-year-old Stashek, to crawl into the back of the oven and cough loudly whenever Srulek (as she called Srulki) started coughing, and not to stop until he did. This was so her friends, neighbors, and all other visiting people would think that her Marinka and Stashek had bad colds and that to get rid of their colds, she was keeping them in a warm place. This way, no one would suspect that she was helping a Jew to get well.

Now, after ten days in her house getting good care, she brought him down to our *kriuvka*. Seeing another Jew for the first time in four months since we escaped *Judenrein* in Frampol was a new kind of experience. When Mrs. Kowalik first told us of another Jew coming to hide with us, we all became suspicious. Maybe she was sending down a man to kill us, since she didn't believe in killing people herself. But when Srulki came down to our place, we all burst into tears. Then we each gave him a hug. That first day none of us spoke. We just lay under the hay-filled cover, Srulki lying next to my brother Joshua. Everyone was sad. We all knew that we had lost our loved ones and that survival was a very long shot.

The next day we began to see one another a bit more clearly, with some light coming through the cracks in the foundation. My mother turned to Srulki and asked him how his family perished. He hesitated to talk. But when he started, Mama warned him to keep his voice down to a whisper. He must never use his normal voice here. He stared at each of us before he started to pour his heart out. He told us about all the atrocities he had witnessed and all the hardships he and his sister Chancia had gone through. When he talked about how he left his sister to die and how he had gotten here, he began to cry. He said he felt very guilty for leaving Chancia to be murdered.

I then touched his hand and said, "You see, Srulki, I also left my sister Perele on the field, shot in a leg. Her leg was bleeding, and she urged me to run again. She was buried in a mass grave, most likely while she was still alive. Mrs. Kowalik told us about these huge graves with so many Jewish men, women, and children buried, many still alive and begging, after Frampol was made *Judenrein*. Now I too am crying, riddled with guilt."

"Save yourselves from feeling guilty," said Mama. "None of us will live much longer to tell about it, so you won't have to deal with the guilt. We are only prolonging the agony," Mama said with a sad voice.

As the days and weeks passed, we all felt closer to Srulki. He was very likeable. And so our existence in the *kriuvka* continued. The cold weather subsided somewhat now that it was March. Our hunger pains, though, continued the same as before. All Maria Kowalik did was fill the pot with two or three more potatoes in the skin for Srulki.

One day Mrs. Kowalik asked Srulki, "Aren't you a tailor?"

"Yes, ma'am," answered Srulki.

My mother understood Maria's question to Srulki, so she added, "He is a very good tailor, Mrs. Kowalik."

The next day Mrs. Kowalik brought down bundles of black and gray material that Mr. Zlomainsky had given her. She also brought down needles and thread, scissors, and a measuring tape. Now Srulki was becoming busy, sewing by hand. He made slacks and jackets for the Kowalik boys as well as for her son-in-law, Chaika, who still didn't know about us, the Jews, hidden away. She told him she bought these things in the town of Yanov.

We each became involved doing something useful to help Srulki with the sewing. My specialty was threading his needles in the dark. Srulki would sit very close to the cracks in the stone foundation, slightly bent, in order to be able to see what he was doing. But shortly after he began sewing, there was no more work for us. Srulki, however, was very busy. The rest of us wished we could also be useful. Maybe it would take our minds off the awful state we were in.

One night when I took the food from Mrs. Kowalik, Mama was right by my side asking Maria Kowalik if she had any yarn and knitting needles. "We can knit for you and your children – sweaters, stockings, mittens, and scarves," said Mama.

"Well . . ." Maria thought for a minute. "Not a bad idea," she replied. "I have some cotton yarn, and maybe I can get some wool skeins with Zlomainsky's help," said skinny Mrs. Kowalik.

So we too became a bit busy. I learned how to knit and crochet very quickly. I was eager to be useful. I lay awake for hours at night trying to think up new and interesting patterns for sweaters. During the day I would first practice my pattern with two knitting needles, then I would show it to the others for approval. If they liked my new design, I would rip out the sample and we'd start a sweater with my design. Oh, that felt good! I began to feel a little important. Even Josh had a job. His task was to untangle the pieces of yarn, tie them together, and roll them into a ball.

Between our knitting and Srulki's sewing, the Kowalik family started looking well-dressed. Soon their friends and neighbors began asking questions. "Where do you get these nice things – suits, sweaters, gloves, stockings, and scarves?" they wondered.

At first Mrs. Kowalik made up stories, such as that she had rich relatives in Yanov and in Warsaw that were sending all these things. But the outsiders' suspicions and questions continued. "When did you last see your rich relatives? Where in Warsaw do they live? How do they send these pretty things? By mail or with other people?" Then a woman asked Mrs. Kowalik in church, "Are you sure you are not hiding Jews somewhere? Jews," she said, "have good skills and could make all kinds of pretty things like you are getting from your relatives in Warsaw."

Maria Kowalik panicked. Soon after Easter she stopped our supply of materials for knitting and sewing. Once in awhile, she would give Srulki enough material to make one pair of pants or one jacket. Also, she occasionally gave us enough yarn to make one scarf or one pair of gloves. She said she couldn't get much more material or yarn. She also told us that she was plain scared. And so our existence under the floor in our hideout continued. Our spirits were low. We were sad souls. Most of our time was now spent lying down under that dirty, scratchy hay cover in complete silence.

Some days Josh and Janice would talk in a whisper about the good old days. They talked about the times when we were free to live, about the good food we used to eat. My mouth would be watering. "Remember the good cookies Bubbie Shaindel used to treat us to?" said Janice.

"Remember how Mama used to bake good challah for the Sabbath and make gefilte fish and chicken soup with knaidlach (matzoh balls), chicken with carrot tzimmes, and such good honey cakes!" said Josh.

They would go on and on. Sometimes Mama just couldn't take it, and she would scold them and call them gluttons. "All you two are talking about is food and the good old times. Stop it!" she scolded them. "Learn from your little sister, Naomi." Mama pointed at me. "She doesn't talk about food all the time like you two. Therefore, Naomi isn't as hungry as you are."

"Oh, Mama," I thought, "if you only knew how hollow my stomach feels. If you only knew how famished I feel all the time. Yes, all the time!" But I lay there not uttering a word. I wanted Mama to think that I was her best child, so she would always keep me near her. "Minnak," I whispered as I lay close to her, holding her bare breast in my hand. Mama's breast was getting smaller all the time. I realized that Mama had lost a lot of weight.

It was now April 1943. Maria Kowalik came down one day and said that Mr. Zlomainsky had told her in church that there was an uprising in the Warsaw ghetto. He told her that when the Germans got ready to liquidate the ghetto and send all the Jews from the ghetto to camps, the Jews knew that no one ever returned or was ever seen alive again from these camps. So somehow they acquired rifles, guns, and other kinds of weapons, and they were fighting with all their might, killing many Germans.

"Please keep us informed about the uprising in the Warsaw ghetto," said Mama to Mrs. Kowalik. "I'll do my best," she replied and left us.

We all looked at Mama, including Srulki. We looked for hope in her face. "Hmmm. Very interesting," said Mama. "Jews are actually able to fight back and are killing Germans in Warsaw!" I could actually see a spark of interest in Mama's face that hadn't been there for a long time.

"Mama," I asked, "does that mean that there is hope that the Jews will win from the Germans and the war will end so we can live and be free?" I could hear Josh and Janice giggle quietly, like mice, at my ignorant question at the age of ten. Srulki had a sick-looking grin on his face as I looked his way.

But Mama turned to me and said, "No, *mein Kindt*. The Jews are not at war with the Germans or with any other nation. The Germans are at war with practically the whole world. We, the Jews, are not a nation. We are scattered all over the world as a people who happen to be Jewish. We are citizens of Poland just like the Kowaliks, Zlomainskys, and many others. They are Christian citizens of Poland, and until Germany occupied Poland, we were also citizens, but Jewish."

"So," I said, "if we, the Jewish people, are not harming anybody – and we are certainly not harming the Germans – why are they not allowing us to live? Why are they so anxious to hunt us down and kill us as if we were their worst enemy? Why, Mama? Why?"

"Here she goes again with her inquisitive head," said Mama sadly. "I've told you before, I don't have the answers. It's God's will, I guess."

"Yes," I said. "Daddy used to say 'It's been decided in the heavens that the Jews of Europe must now die, and God must have his reasons for that, but we are not worthy of knowing his reasons. So we must accept our fate without question.'"

Since I saw that Mama was still in a talkative mood, I took advantage and continued to ask some more. "Mama," I said, "What if we became Christians? Would Hitler and the others let us live?"

"No, Naomi, they wouldn't. Hitler wants even those Christians whose grandparents were Jewish dead. You remember Mr. Golombak's wife from Goray?" asked Mama.

"Yes, I do," I replied.

"Well, they killed her too because her mother's mother was Jewish and converted to Christianity. To the Germans she had Jewish roots, Jewish blood."

Mama was getting upset as she continued to give me a bleak lesson in Jewish history. "You know many German Jews were assimilated," said Mama. "They didn't practice Judaism, but to Hitler and his people, they were Jewish, just the same as we are." Mama looked at me, and continued, "During the Spanish Inquisition in the fifteenth century, Spain gave the Jews a choice – to either convert to Christianity or be expelled from Spain. If a Jew was found studying the Talmud, he would be shot."

"How interesting," I thought. I used to hear people talk about a Spanish Inquisition, but I'd never known what that meant until now.

"Now," Mama concluded sadly, "we have no choices."

Every few days Mrs. Kowalik or her older children would travel to Goray to sell some of their farm products, such as milk, cheese, butter, eggs, and sacks filled with wheat and barley, to the townspeople. All these mouth-watering things that she never gave us a taste of! It made me mad. But I always had to remember Mama's words, "She's a good woman; she risks her life and her family's lives in keeping us here." So I tried not to think about it too much.

In town they found out more about the uprising in the Warsaw ghetto. For a couple of weeks, we kept hearing from the Kowaliks that the Jews were still victorious in killing Germans who came close to the ghetto walls. But eventually the Germans bombed the ghetto and destroyed everything and everyone in it. No more Jews in Warsaw either. The news of the destruction of the Warsaw ghetto was very depressing and disturbing. We had a lengthy discussion about the Warsaw ghetto uprising. Srulki wished he had been there. At least, he felt, he could have killed some Germans in retaliation for killing so many of our people – innocent victims! Mama was very curious about how the Jews of Warsaw acquired so many weapons. "At least," she said, "they were able to fight back and kill some of our worst enemy since time began."

This discussion made me more nervous. I feared that Mama, Srulki, and Janice might decide to go fight the Germans in order to die a heroic death. I just wanted to survive and then have our revenge by seeing that all of Germany was destroyed but that we lived on as heroes they had failed to annihilate. I used to lie in the *kriuvka* dreaming of the possibility that we would be freed. Free to live like other people! And somehow I knew we would come to America if we were free, and I would see myself standing on a bench and telling my story to the American people. The people would listen very closely to my story. They would want to know it all from me, and I would tell them everything. Of course, in 1943 it was just that – only a dream.

Stashek, the youngest of Mrs. Kowalik's sons, once brought our potatoes for the day. As I opened the two boards and looked inside the pot, I became angry. The pot was half empty. "What happened?" I asked. "Why only half a pot of potatoes today?"

"Well, you see," said Stashek, "as I was walking down the hill, I was swinging the pot back and forth, and some of the potatoes just kept falling out of the pot."

But before I could say anything else, he threatened me by saying that if I mentioned this to his mother, he would give us out to the village sheriff, and the sheriff would make soap out of us. "You know that's what they do to Jews now. They make soap out of you," he said. "So you'd better keep quiet, and you might live to go to America." (Even Stashek knew about Jews dreaming of surviving and immigrating to America.) "But when you get to America, you'd better send me a bicycle. You hear me? You promise?" he kept asking.

"Yes, I promise, we promise," I said to him, hardly believing this dream would ever come true. The next twenty-four hours was even harder to endure than usual, with only one and a half potatoes instead of the three medium potatoes or two large ones that we usually got.

One evening in April we got a pot of beans instead of potatoes. I was excited, lowering myself down to our nest and whispering happily, "Look everybody, look, we have beans tonight! Beans instead of potatoes – isn't it great?"

Mama took the pot of beans from me and said, "I know how much all of you would like to devour these beans, but we can't have them. We have to bury them right away."

"But why, Mama? Why?" We each asked in as loud a whisper as we were allowed.

"You see, children, today is the second day of our holiday, Passover, and Jews are not permitted to eat bread or certain other things, such as beans. It's true," said Mama. "We have to live like animals in order to try to survive. But we are human, and we must not let go of our laws, our traditions, as long as we live and breathe."

"But Mama," asked Josh, "how do you still know that it's a Jewish holiday? After all these months in hiding without a Jewish calendar?"

Mama answered, with some little pride, "Take my word for it, son. If by some miracle we should survive this horrible war, you will see that your mother has a built-in calendar in her head."

Reluctantly, Srulki and Josh made a hole in the ground with their hands and buried the beans. And we went without food another day.

I also remember seeing through the cracks between the two boards as Mrs. Kowalik's maid, Wanda, and her twelve-year-old daughter sat at a wooden table eating their lunch. Usually their lunch consisted of bread, cheese, and milk – as much as she and her daughter could eat and drink. One day, watching Wanda and her daughter eat their lunch, I turned to Mama, who often sat beside me, and said, "If I could live and be free, I would never ask for more than to be a maid, eat bread as much as I want, and drink milk as much as I want to."

"You forgot the cheese," Mama teased me.

"Oh, Mama, I want to be outside and look up at the beautiful sky, lie on the grass and . . . and . . ."

"And what?" asked Mama.

"Play with my friends!" I cried, knowing they were all dead.

I also remember, one summer day, looking out and seeing the four Kowalik boys eating cereal cooked in milk. They were spooning out the cereal from a black iron pot. "Look, Mama," I said. "They are eating grits cooked in milk. Yummm," I drooled. As we both looked, we saw them enjoying their cereal.

Then we heard Bronek, the second son, saying, as they neared the end of the food in the pot, "If you want to bring Mother a clean pot, watch this. I'll throw the pot to the Jews for five minutes, and I guarantee you they will clean the pot to the last grit."

When Mama heard Bronek's words, she quickly disappeared down to our nest. But Janice, Josh, Srulki, and I did exactly what Bronek predicted we would do. We scraped the pot clean with our fingernails. I even put the pot over my head and licked the very bottom clean. Then we returned the pot to Bronek, who was waiting with his brothers at the boards. I handed him the pot, and all four of them had a good laugh. Mama didn't cry as much these days. But when she saw her children turned into animals, tears just ran from her eyes.

The summer of 1943 was a long and difficult period for us. It seemed as if the war would never end. Our spirits were sagging, and our bodies were becoming more frail. We didn't hear any encouraging news through the Kowaliks from Mr. Zlomainsky or from any other sources. The cities, towns, and villages were all made Judenrein. Except for the concentration camps, there were no more Jews to do the hard labor for the Germans. So now the Germans started drafting young and able-bodied Polish men to do the work that Jews once did. They needed men to dig ditches, repair small bridges mined by the underground Partisans, and do other hard labor.

Mrs. Kowalik's two oldest sons, Yanek, age twenty, and Bronek, age nineteen, were drafted to do *zwanks arbeit* (forced labor). They worked for one week, and then they escaped. When the Germans came to look for them, they came to hide in our *kriuvka*, lying on their stomachs. Since they were tall men, they really couldn't sit under the floor. Yanek and Bronek kept looking at us and asking questions. "Why are you staying here? It smells so bad. Why don't you comb your hair?" Bronek asked me.

"I have no comb," I answered him.

"No comb?" he said. "Too bad!" They would look at us and then look at each other and start laughing.

Just then we heard the Germans in the courtyard and in the empty barn about ten feet from our hiding place, yelling and warning Mrs. Kowalik to see that her sons returned to the forced labor as soon as possible, or else! Mrs. Kowalik didn't understand German and neither did the sheriff, but they somehow knew that the Germans had given them a warning.

We Jews understood most of what the Germans said, and we explained to Yanek and to Bronek after the Germans and the sheriff left. Yanek and Bronek looked at us again. They said that we smelled worse than the pigs. As they were beginning to crawl out, Yanek turned around and said, "Jesus Christus, I would rather die than have to live like you do for one week."

"I know," said my mother. "I hope you never have to be tried. Not even for one week."

About a month or so later, Yanek and Bronek escaped again. This time they went into the forest to hide when they got word from a friend that the Germans were coming to look for them. The Germans came with an interpreter. We could hear their angry voices when they came into the barn about ten feet away from us. They were shouting at Mrs. Kowalik and her daughter Juzefka. One of the few words Juzefka knew in German was Jawol (yes). She later told us that she kept saying "Jawol" so that we could hear her voice and know that the Germans were still on their property.

"Maybe they are hiding under this floor," said one German, banging on it with his rifle.

"Let's remove some boards and see," said another one.

As they started chopping up the floor with a hatchet – eight to ten feet from us – we all felt that this was finally our end. Mama looked at each of us with her finger on her lips, as if to say, "Keep silent." But Josh couldn't stop shaking so hard his teeth were chattering.

We now saw a hand lifting up a piece of board. At this point Mama stretched over to Josh. She put one of her hands in Josh's mouth to stop the chattering, and then she wrapped the fingers of her other hand around his neck. By the look on her face, you could see she was warning Josh to stop shaking, or she'd have to strangle him. It may sound unreal, but it worked. He stopped shaking.

"Look," said one German to the other, "the nails in this piece of board are rusty. I guess they wouldn't be hiding here."

When Maria Kowalik saw them chopping the floor, she passed out and fell to the ground. "What is with her?" asked one Nazi.

"She has a bad heart and she faints all the time," said Juzefka.

"Are you sure we aren't getting close to where your brothers are?" asked another.

"No, sir," answered Juzefka. "My brothers are not at home."

Eventually, when they had all left the Kowalik property, Mama loosened her hand from Josh's throat and took her bleeding fingers out of his mouth, and we all started to be reborn. The terrible panic started to subside, and we just lay there in complete silence, trying to breathe in and out. We worried about Mrs. Kowalik's fainting and wondered how she was doing. That evening Mama decided to crawl up to pick up the potatoes. When Mama saw Juzefka, sad and angry, holding the pot, Mama asked, "How is your mother, Juzefka?"

"She's sick in bed," grumbled Juzefka. "Thanks to you Jews, she almost died today when she saw the Germans breaking into the floor. She was so sure they'd find you. You know what they would do to us if they found you here?" answered Juzefka, trying to rush away from Mama.

Mama took her hand quickly before she got away and said to her, "Tell your mother we are praying to God for her good health. You will see, Juzefka, your mother will get well very soon."

"I wish you would also pray to our Lord Jesus," said Juzefka. "But you are Jewish, and you only pray to God, and not to his holy son, Jesus." Juzefka crossed herself as she turned and ran toward her home.

Maria Kowalik got better, but she avoided seeing us for some time. Her children took turns bringing us the potatoes in the evening. I would see Mrs. Kowalik through the crack. She was doing her work, moving around, but she was not as fast or frisky as she used to be before she fainted.

One night in late August of 1943, Maria Kowalik herself came with the pot of potatoes and decided to crawl down to our nest with the lantern in hand. "Bad news," whispered Mama.

Sure enough, Maria started by saying that she couldn't and she wouldn't keep us any longer. "There is no end in sight to this long and bitter war. You have been here for many months. I live in constant fear that they will find you here," she continued. "You are Jews. You have to die. I can't risk my life and the lives of my children because of you. So, leave! Go, get out of here! And, Faiga, don't give me that speech about your children's blood on my conscience. I can't and I won't listen to that any longer. This is the last time you will get food from me," she concluded.

We listened to her words, all of us in great shock. My mother didn't seem to be able to find the right words to say, so she was quiet for awhile. That really threw me into a panic. "Is Mama giving up?" I thought. "Are we really going to die?"

But Mama did start talking. And this is what she said to Maria: "My dear Mrs. Kowalik, what you just said is all true. We have created a problem for you from the first moment you took pity on us and put us in hiding on your property. But you see how determined we are to survive to tell our story to the free world. To tell the world that among so many bad, mean, and vicious people, we found a real good person. We found you, who did take pity on us. Not only did you have a good heart, but you were willing to take a chance, and with God's help, you might just succeed in saving five – not one or two but five – lives. Think about that."

"No," Maria said. "No, don't talk to me like that! I can't take it! I do have a sick heart, you know; and I might just die and leave you, my problem, to my children. I can't do that."

"You won't die, Maria. You will live to be a very old lady. You'll see. God's reward will come your way."

"I can't keep you any longer or give you any more food, even though it isn't much. I just can't give it to you. We're in a bad war, and many of our Christian people are starving, too," she said.

Now Mama continued, "You know that we never complained to

you, living outside all winter in the bitterest of weather. These children and Srulki nearly starve all the time. But we are not asking, nor do we expect, more from you. I know it's hard for you. But just let us stay, and you'll see, no one will ever hear us or see us moving around. And I do appeal to your conscience to try to save these children's lives. Enough children have already died at the hands of these German murderers."

"No, no!" Maria was now even more upset and angry. "You either leave or I'll starve you here in this hole in the ground!"

"So go ahead, starve us until we die a slow death." Mama raised her voice but still spoke in a whisper.

"On second thought, Maria," said Mama. "If I see you are really letting us die of starvation, we will leave here and we will give ourselves up. But before the German murderers shoot us, I will tell them about how you once had pity on us Jews, and how you once thought of us as human beings, and how you hid us and fed us for nine long months. So you might as well take a gun, Mrs. Kowalik, and get it over with. Shoot us! Kill us, and your worries will be over." Mama's voice was desperate.

Maria Kowalik was beside herself. She just turned away from us, fuming, and out she went in a rage. Srulki crawled up the short tunnel and closed the two boards. When he came back, he asked my mother if he should try his luck and join the Partisans.

"What Partisans?" said Mama. "Don't you know that the Partisans in the woods around here are the biggest anti-Semites? They will do to you what they did to poor Pesach. They used him for awhile, and then they shot him. His body was found around here in the spring."

"That's true," answered Srulki. "I thought it might be easier for you if I left."

"No," said Mama. "Don't go wandering around anymore. We'll just have to wait and see. And whatever happens, happens."

Mama's last sentence disturbed me even more, and I now worried more than before. Lying under the cover with my knees close to my chest – I'd gotten used to this position in the winter in order to keep from freezing – I began to wait for tomorrow, hoping the potatoes would come and that life in the *kriuvka* would continue. But the next evening came, and there was no sign of anybody knocking on our boards. Still hoping late into the night, we were all tuned to the sounds outside. But no potatoes. The horrible thoughts that went through my mind made me forget the hunger. The thick silence in the *kriuvka* was deafening for another twenty-four hours.

The next evening there was that familiar knock on the boards. I leaped into the tunnel and opened the boards. Marinka Kowalik, who was my age, stood there with a pot of potatoes in her hands. She handed me the pot, staring into my eyes as I stared into hers. "She's ten years old, like me." I thought. "But she is free and I'm not. I must hide."

▬▬

One evening in September of 1943, as I crawled down to our nest carrying the potatoes, I heard Mama quietly humming a familiar tune. I used to hear Mama praying with that tune on Jewish High Holidays in the synagogue. She was humming that tune and sobbing at the same time. I put the food down next to Mama. She was sitting bent forward. The floor above us was touching the back of her head as she continued crying.

"Children," said Mama. "It's Rosh Hashanah Eve."

I knew that Rosh Hashanah and Yom Kippur were usually in September, but I just hadn't thought about it until now. "Faiga, are you sure it's Rosh Hashanah?" asked Srulki. Srulki had not realized that my mother had an exceptional memory for dates. He didn't know that Mama knew all the secular dates, and especially knew and kept track of the Jewish dates, without a written calendar. So if Mama says it's Rosh Hashanah, then we know that the High Holidays are upon us.

"Last year," whispered Janice, "things were already very bad for the Jews in the ghettos. But we were still a complete family in our own home in Goray."

"Oh, yes," I thought. "We were still a complete and shining menorah." Of course, the day after Rosh Hashanah in 1942 the big fire had started in Goray and my hometown had become Judenrein. Now we were hiding in Mrs. Kowalik's *kriuvka* in the village of Lada, and we were about to pray together to God, asking him to grant us all another year of life. All five of us huddled together, arms around each other, and cried as we prayed. Each of us prayed with his or her own thoughts. Until we died, our thoughts were the one thing the enemies could not take away from us...

My thoughts took me back a few years. In my thoughts, I was in our synagogue on Rosh Hashanah, sitting on a bench in the back of the women's section, dangling my legs back and forth while eating some goodies that Mama brought along to keep me busy and quiet while the grownups followed the cantor in prayer. My mother had a place at the eastern wall, looking down into the men's section. She had a very melodious voice, and she knew all the prayers very well. My father used to say that my mother *davened* (prayed) like a *chazzan* (cantor).

As a child, I always liked the story that my bubbie Shaindel used to tell us about how, when my mother became of school age, my zaida sent her to a boys' *cheder* (Hebrew school) to study Torah and to learn all the prayers that the boys her age learned. It was an unusual way to educate a girl. But Mama was the oldest child in her home, and her only sister, Hudel, was twelve years younger. Bubbie told us that my mother would sit in *cheder* on the opposite side of the classroom from the boys, and that she learned very well. She caught on quickly. "She was the best in *cheder*," Bubbie would say. "She just loved studying Bible."

When Mama used to pray in the synagogue, she would always have a group of women around her, listening to her chanting the prayers like a cantor. Mama knew that she was not to disturb the cantor and the men, so she kept her voice lower than she would have liked to. My mother was known in *shul* (synagogue) as the "ladies' cantor." I remember how Mama would call me over at a certain time during the service on Rosh Hashanah and Yom Kippur. She would point in her *machzer* (High Holiday prayer book) and say to me, "This is one of the most important prayers on this holiday, so listen, Naomi. It is called the 'Unesana Tokef.' Here it says that on Rosh Hashanah, the Lord inscribes our fate. And on Yom Kippur, the Day of Atonement, the decree is sealed. How many shall pass away this year, and how many shall be born. Who shall live, and who shall die. Who shall perish by fire, and who by drowning. Who will die by the sword, and who will die from hunger or from thirst. Who will die being strangled, and who will die being stoned to death. Who shall go wandering, and who shall stay at home. Who shall be tranquil, and who shall be harassed."

As a young child, I pretended to be serious about that prayer, but in reality, it didn't mean much to me at the time. It did make me somewhat aware of death. And I would think that someday my grandparents would die, because they were in their sixties – and to me, that was old. It also made me think that in a very far away time, my parents would become very old, and they too would die. But I refused to worry about that when I was only five, six, or seven years old. About my own mortality? Well, that seemed like millions of years away. "If and when I ever die," I would think, "I will be very, very old – so old that I'll just go to sleep and die, and go straight to heaven."

At a very young age, all I wanted was to be with my friends and play imaginary games. At home I used to watch my older sisters do their homework after school. They would read, write, do arithmetic, and memorize poems. I would listen to the poems in Polish and memorize them too. My sisters also attended Bais Ya'akov, a school for girls, in the afternoon. I always liked going along to Bais Ya'akov with them. And since Bais Ya'akov School was only a few years old and wasn't yet well organized, it was all right for me to come along with my older sisters, as long as I promised to behave. At Bais Ya'akov, I would learn some Hebrew songs as well as *brachos* (blessings). At home I mimicked my sisters in the morning, saying the morning prayer called *Modeh Ani*. At night, I learned the prayer called *Shema Yisrael*. Once my sister Janice asked me if I wanted to learn a Yiddish prayer before bedtime. She told me that it was a very nice prayer that every child should say at bedtime. Since it was in Yiddish and not Hebrew, I would be able to understand and appreciate its meaning. (Yiddish was the language we were born into and spoke in our house.) The prayer in Yiddish went like this:

Ich vell gut zein, Ich vell frum zein.
Ich vell tun vas Got geboten haut.
Vas mein Tota hayst, vas mein Moma hayst,
Vas alle gutte un frumeh leit haysen mich tun,
Tzum gutten vell Ich tun.
A brocha un hatzlachah zol kummen,
Oif mir un mein kepele.
Omen, selah.
[I will be good, I will be observant.

I will do what God has commanded me to do.
What my father asks of me and what my mother wants me to do
What all good and pious people tell me to do
I will happily do all the good things. And in return I hope
A blessing and success should come to me and to my little head.
Amen, Selah.

Now it was Rosh Hashanah 1943, and everything that I didn't take seriously when I was younger, plus all the horrors that had happened in the past two years, were facing me at age ten. The worst horror was that I might never live to be eleven. I was facing death from hunger or from frost. We were all facing death, perhaps from some dreaded disease that could come to us in this most unsanitary nest. We might all die by the sword if the Kowalik boys decided to slaughter us. Or we might all die from the dreaded bullets, at the hands of the German murderers or Polish collaborators.

And yet, in the midst of our crying while in our huddle, we wished each other "Shanah tovah," a good year. "Shanah metukah," a sweet year. "Shanah mevurechet," a year filled with blessings. And, of course, we wished each other "Shnat chaim," a year of life.

September 1943 was a month of anxiety, tension, and worry for us. We worried about what Maria Kowalik would do with us. Would she really continue bringing us the pot of potatoes and let us stay? Or would she force us to leave the *kriuvka*? Or would she starve us to death right here? I was mostly worried about Mama's idea that she might as well kill us with her rifle and get it over with. I didn't want it to be over with. I wanted to live and be free one day soon. When the familiar knock would come on the boards in the evenings, and I was expected to go get the pot of potatoes, I would get a frightened feeling inside my stomach. "What if Maria is standing there with a rifle in her hands instead of a pot of potatoes?" I thought. For a few seconds, I lay frozen with fear inside me. Then I would hear Mama say, "What's with you, Naomi? Get moving and bring our food down!"

In September the weather was still warm. I would spend some of the days just sitting curled up with my hands hugging my legs below my knees, bringing my knees up to my chin and looking out through the cracks between the two boards. Through these cracks I would see part of the activities in the courtyard. I could see Juzefka throwing grain to the chickens. I sometimes saw cows and pigs getting their treats from the trough. I prayed they wouldn't finish it all. Maybe Mama would let us go out later at night, and we could fill ourselves up on their leftovers. Mama was now extra cautious that somebody shouldn't spot us and watch us go to our hiding place. So sometimes Mama said no, and we had to listen to her. Through the cracks I would still see some of the Kowaliks, or Wanda the maid, with her twelve-year-old daughter, eating lunch at the wooden table and benches. I just stared, drooled, and waited for the days to go by. At night I would crawl under the hay cover and curl up. If I was lucky, I would be tired enough to fall asleep.

"I'm coming in with you, Helena," said Mrs. Kowalik as she handed me the pot of potatoes on a Sunday evening in late September 1943.

"More bad news about Jews being tortured and killed," I thought to myself. Whenever Maria Kowalik put her lantern in front of her and came crawling down to our *kriuvka*, it meant bad news.

Sure enough, she started out by telling my mother a story that she heard at church in Goray. She looked at Mama most of the time when she talked. That morning, when she and her children arrived in church, people were crying, wiping their eyes, and talking about losing a young Polish man named Mietek because he was hiding a Jewish girl he intended to marry after the war. The nineteen-year-old girl was Goldie, Reuven the baker's daughter. Mietek, they said, was very much in love with Goldie.

A year before, when Goray became *Judenrein*, Mietek had hidden Goldie in the attic of his parents' house. Goldie remained hidden during the day. At night she would come down to eat at the table in the house. Mietek made sure to close all the shutters and curtains so no one could see her from the outside. But two young sisters who lived next door with their family found a way, through a little opening, to see Goldie in their neighbors' house. The sisters, it seemed, had a crush on the handsome Mietek and became very jealous of Goldie. So they reported to the Germans that the twenty-one-year-old gentile was harboring a Jew.

Last Tuesday, Maria said, several Germans burst into Mietek's house. They grabbed him, dragged Goldie down from the attic, and arrested both of them. They were to be killed at sundown. Mietek's mother rushed to the jailhouse to plead for her son's life. She bribed the Nazis not to kill her son. They agreed. They told her that at sundown they would take both prisoners out of jail. They would shoot and kill the Jewish woman but would shoot to the side of Mietek. She should tell her son to fall to the ground and pretend to be dead. Then, when all the spectators had gone and it was dark, Mietek should escape to another city far away, never to return.

The mother rushed to the jail where Mietek and Goldie were locked behind bars to tell her son the good news. Mietek listened and then told his mother to go back to the German murderers and try to bribe them again, asking them to agree to pretend they were killing *both* him and Goldie. Then, when it got dark, they would both escape. Mietek told his mother that without Goldie's love he couldn't go on living. His life had meaning only because he had Goldie.

Mietek's mother realized how much Goldie meant to her son, so she went to see the Germans with more money and some of her jewelry, and she begged on her knees to let them both escape. At first the Germans shouted that they could never let a Jew escape. Then, after talking to each other in German, one of the SS men told her to bring more money. So she returned with more money, borrowed from her relatives and friends. When she handed the money over, they told her to take off her gold earrings and hand them over too. Mietek's mother did as the SS men instructed her. Very excited, she ran to the jail to tell her son and Goldie the good news. She kissed Mietek and Goldie through the iron bars and said to them, "We'll meet again after the war. May God watch over you until then!"

When it got dark, a crowd gathered near the jailhouse. Goldie and Mietek were led out of jail. Hand-in-hand, the two stood against the wall. Several shots were heard. Mietek and Goldie fell to the ground. One SS man turned to the crowd and told them to take a lesson today. He told them that what happened today to this nice young Polish gentile could happen to any one of them if they hid Jews.

When everyone was gone, Mietek's mother rushed over to the jail wall, expecting to find her son Mietek and Goldie gone. But to her painful and horrified surprise, she found them both shot to death and lying in a pool of their own blood. Mietek's mother ran hysterically to the priest and told him the whole story.

"Yesterday," said Mrs. Kowalik, "this poor woman buried her son and Goldie, the woman her son loved so much and gave his life for, in one grave, right in front of her house." Maria Kowalik told us that she and her children went to see the grave after church.

She and many other passers-by put flowers on the grave of the two people in love.

We listened with great interest and with panic inside. As Mrs. Kowalik and Mama continued to talk a while longer, my mind began wandering, thinking about what terrible things would eventually happen to us. As Maria Kowalik was leaving us, she stopped crawling midway. Holding on to her lantern, she turned around, looked at us, and said, "I must be crazy!"

October came, and with it came the rains. We were still in hiding – Mrs. Kowalik and her children had not killed us. During these rainy days, we spent most of our days and nights under the gray, dirty hay cover. The conditions in the kriuvka were worse than ever. I lay cuddled up in a fetal position all the time. Sometimes I sucked on my bony knees that were close to my face. The damp, cold weather had started to set in. I would scratch myself all over. I was always peeling off the scabs from sores that became dry and crusty on my body and my scalp. Lice and other vermin nestled in my hair and on other sores all over my body. I put my fingers in my hair to scratch and remove some scabs. My fingernails often opened wounds on my head, and my hand would come out bloody. I wiped the blood off with the gray shirt I had now been wearing for more than half a year. Lately, I'd become more sad than I'd been so far. But our life – or should I say, our existence – continued in the kriuvka.

November 2, 1943, made it one full year since Frampol became Judenrein. We had now been hiding out for one full year, and we didn't hear any encouraging news about the war coming to an end anytime soon. The days, although they were shorter now, went by very slowly and seemed very long and depressing. Most of the time now, I was lying next to Mama. My hand now automatically went inside to Mama's chest. I felt anger at Mama because she hardly had a breast for me to hold and find some comfort. I wanted to call her "Minnak," but my lips were closed tight. I just couldn't get myself to express love to my mother. Hope was now a vague thought. Every day my feelings were dying a little more. Numbness was setting in. The will to live was no longer as strong.

I tried to divert my thoughts to some of the good old days, the days I spent with friends. Days together with family. It was hard to make myself forget the state we were in. The feeling of hopelessness was really bad. But I tried. Hard as it was, I began to think of the holidays and the Sabbath, when our store was closed and the family would all be together. I thought of how I used to walk with my mother on the Sabbath to our synagogue. Mama let me carry her prayer book and her pretty silk handkerchief with a cookie for me wrapped inside it. I was holding Mama's hand and looking up at her. Mama was dressed in a beautiful Sabbath dress and wearing her three strands of cultured pearls on her long and graceful neck. Mama's friends used to kid her and say that she had a neck like a giraffe – perfect for wearing lots of pearls! My father had given her these pearls as a gift, and she loved wearing them on good and happy occasions. I thought my mother was the most beautiful woman in town. When I walked hand in hand with my mother, I thought everybody in town stared at us. I thought I was the envy of the girls in Goray to have such a beautiful mother.

On Sabbath afternoons in the summer, I would accompany my mother to her friends' houses, where I would always get cake and candy from the hostess. Boy, did I like that! Mama had a lively bunch of friends who would talk about many subjects. Some of Mama's friends would tell interesting stories. I was curious, and I always listened. Sometimes they talked about their husbands and about sex. When I would ask my mother what all that meant, she would always answer me, "You are too young to understand. Some day when you grow up, I will explain it all to you. For now, have some candy."

That was fine with me – I loved candy! But I always wondered what they were whispering and laughing about. Mama and her friends seemed so happy and always seemed to have a good time being together. Now, hiding out in the foundation of the Kowaliks' barns, I longed for those good old days when I was five, six, seven, and even eight.

December arrived with the most snowstorms and the bitterest cold we had ever experienced. The stormy winds blew in cold air and snow through the small cracks between the stones of the foundation. We tried to close these cracks by pushing in some hay and straw, but the wind was fierce and blew the stuffing right back on us. We would crawl under the cover completely, heads and all, and just lie there waiting until the storms were over.

One evening when the knock on the boards came and I opened up, Oleshek Kowalik was holding the pot in his hands and a round loaf of bread under his arm. Oleshek, age fifteen, was Maria Kowalik's third son and fifth child. He was always pleasant to us. "Here," he said, handing me the pot of potatoes. Then he gave me the bread. "It's New Year's Eve," he said, "so enjoy!"

"Thank you so very much," I said, bowing my head.

"Someday you will send me a *bzytef* [straight shaving razor] from America," he said. "Don't forget I asked for it. I'm now old enough to shave."

"Of course, sir, we will send you a *bzytef*," I answered. But in my heart, I doubted that we would ever live to see America, that we would ever be free.

He stared at me with pity in his eyes. He unbuttoned his coat, took off his scarf, and came close to me as I was holding the food. He put the scarf on my head and wrapped it around my neck. I was too shocked to talk and say "Thank you." He started walking away, and then he turned and said again, "Happy New Year."

Just then I managed to compose myself before he was gone, and I answered him, "Happy New Year to you, and thank you very, very much for the scarf. Thank you! Thank you!" I was still thanking him when he closed the big doors to the courtyard.

"Don't eat the bread all at once," said Mama, as she broke the round rye bread into pieces. She gave each one of us a large chunk and a small piece. "Save some for tomorrow."

We all agreed to save some, but the temptation was too close to our teeth. First, I started to smell my two pieces of bread, and my mouth was watering. I began to play a game. The small piece was my mother's delicious honeycake, I pretended. And the large piece was my favorite ice cream that I used to buy from Chaya Katz. My honeycake I devoured in no time. "Mama," I said, "I just finished your delicious honeycake." Mama understood me, and I felt her squeeze my shoulder. "Now," I said, "I'm going to lick on my ice cream cone that I bought from Chaya Katz. She made the best ice cream in the world, didn't she, Mama?"

"And you were her best customer," replied Mama. "You used to spend every *groshen* you received from your bubbie Shaindel for doing chores for her, and you'd run straight to Chaya Katz's candy store for ice cream. And if Chaya Katz was in the middle of making the ice cream, you sat watching her and her husband churning and turning the ice cream tank back and forth until it became firm ice cream."

"Yes, Mama," I said, "and she let me taste it to see if it was just right!"

I was becoming excited just thinking about how I used to love to go to Chaya Katz's store. Some days my friends and I would buy up all the ice cream, and Chaya Katz would send us home, telling us she now had no more ice cream for her other customers.

"Save some bread for tomorrow," said Mama once again.

"I'll save my potatoes for tomorrow. Tonight, I'm feasting on honeycake and ice cream," I replied. I could almost hear Mama chuckle a bit. Oh, that made me so happy! Because most of the time while in hiding, Mama was very, very sad.

"Tomorrow is 1944, a new year," said Srulki. "Does anybody here think that we will make it to 1945?"

"Of course we will," answered Janice. "We will outlast this world war, and we will all sail to America," she said.

"I think I will go to Palestine," said Srulki. "In Palestine, I will work shoulder to shoulder with other *chalutzim* [pioneers], and I will help build a Jewish land."

"*Kinder* [children]," said my mother, "you are all dreaming. With this monster of a war that we see no end to, and with the odds piled up against us, I'm surprised we are still breathing like human beings."

"But if we pray hard enough to God, a dream can become a reality."

These words were spoken by my brother Joshua. Josh would surprise us when he spoke. He hardly talked at all lately, while in hiding. Now he spent most of his time, when it wasn't freezing - or even colder - praying to God and reading his small book of *Tehillim* (Psalms) that he had managed to hide in his pocket when he escaped *Judenrein*.

"Josh, you live in a world of philosophy and religion. I certainly hope you are right. I hope God hears all our prayers," said Srulki in a sad and low whisper.

January and February 1944 were extremely difficult months to survive in our hiding place. The harsh, cold weather was once again biting at us. Our hunger pains continued. Despair was written all over our thin faces. Many of our companions, like some of the mice and rats, couldn't make it through the bitter frozen ground they were on or in. We would find them lying dead. Lying under that cover and trying to think of the good days gone by was now ever so much more difficult. I just couldn't let myself be teased into thinking of the good old days. But having a human brain, I thought all the time, mostly of the days in the ghetto.

I remembered when people were dispossessed and sent to Goray. We, the Jewish community, had to make room for the dispossessed and take them into our homes. Our house became crowded with people from all over. I remembered sleeping on the floor next to my sister Perele. On my other side was a couple from Germany. Mama said they were newlyweds. (I remember only their last name, Ulman.) At night, Mama gave out as many blankets and pillows as she had. Some people slept uncovered, others had no pillows. When we were lying down on the floor, Mama came over and whispered to the newlyweds, "Behave! Don't forget there is a young child next to you." And Mama pointed at me. I didn't understand what Mama was talking about.

About an hour went by, and the Ulmans must have thought that I was asleep. They embraced each other and were turning from side to side. In no time at all, Mama appeared and scolded the couple. "This is not a private bedroom! There are many young unmarried people in this room. Don't make me have to come over again. If you do, you will sleep outside!" Mama sounded angry. I was wondering what was so wrong with the way they were rocking each other to sleep.

People in the ghetto were always hungry and, in the winter, also cold. The Jewish people couldn't buy wood for their woodburning ovens from gentiles. The ghetto was always guarded by Germans and by some of Stefan Mrożyk's gang. The *akzias* became more and more frequent. People were dying. Some died from hunger, others from frost. The mood of the Jewish people was constantly sagging. If you saw a Jew in the street in 1942, you saw a sad face, perhaps a hungry person worrying about what would happen to him or her.

I remember Mama's cousin, Laibish, who was a barber in Goray. He was tall, husky, and good-looking. But now Laibish was no longer useful. He was very thin and sick in bed. Laibish was now always crying and begging for food. "I'm hungry! Please, people, give me something to eat!" he would cry.

Whenever I went to see my grandparents, I would have to pass down the hall. The door to his room was always open, and he would call out, "I'm hungry, I'm hungry!" I would get some potato soup from my bubbie Shaindel and bring it to him. He would devour the soup and cry again, "I'm hungry, I'm hungry!"

Every day there were funerals in Goray. People were either killed by the Germans or by Mrożyk's boys, or they just died. One day it was the funeral of Laibish, the barber. I felt guilty that I was relieved not to have to hear his haunted cries of "I'm hungry, I'm hungry!" We were all hungry!

The first sibling my father lost at the hands of the German murderers was his younger brother, Chayim. Chayim was a veterinarian who lived with his family in the village of Chshanov Lubelsky, about sixteen to eighteen miles from my hometown of Goray. I remember Uncle Chayim as a very dear uncle. I always looked forward to his visits to our house. His daughter Shprintza, next to the youngest of his children, was my age. He had three other children. Uncle Chayim used to bring us all kinds of goodies from his farm in Chshanov. He would hold up a wrapped piece of candy in his hand and ask me if I knew what blessing one makes before eating candy. I would say the blessing, and Uncle Chayim would act amazed that I knew it and would comment on how smart I was. Then he would hand me the candy. Uncle Chayim always made me feel good.

Uncle Chayim attended to the animals who needed care in the whole village of Chshanov. He treated the cattle, the horses, and all the rest of the animals on the farms. He was loved by the village people, and since they had no doctor in Chshanov, people would call on Uncle Chayim to help them through a sickness. He gave them remedies, and they recovered. If he couldn't handle someone's illness, he'd make sure they would travel to a town and see a physician.

Now, in the spring of 1942, my uncle Chayim lay dead on the wagon in front of our house. His wife, Perel-Ethel, and his four children were crying by his side. They had brought him to Goray to be buried in the cemetery. Uncle Chayim had been shot in the head by German soldiers. We were all in shock. As people gathered around our house, everyone who knew Uncle Chayim was crying. My grandparents, Bubbie Hena and Zaida Yossel, stood over their dead son and wept. My father's four sisters, Ethel, Perel, Chana, and Sara Deena, were all crying and asking, "Why? Why? What did Chayim do to deserve to be killed?" My father's brothers, Zelig and Shimon, were also there crying.

I noticed that the only person who didn't cry was my father. There was pain in his face, but no tears came from his eyes. After awhile we all gathered around Aunt Perel-Ethel and listened to her telling us what really happened. Through the tears streaming down her face, she told us that two German soldiers had stormed into their house, accompanied by a Polish villager. They had angrily informed Uncle Chayim that a comrade of theirs, a third soldier lying in their jeep outside, had been shot in the head on the road from the town of Yanov by the Partisans, who came out of the woods and confronted them. They rushed Uncle Chayim out to see the soldier in the jeep and ordered him to save the soldier's life. If Uncle Chayim didn't save him, they would kill Uncle Chayim, they warned. Uncle Chayim examined the wounded German soldier and told his buddies that their friend was in a coma; he was shot through the brain and beyond any help. In his opinion, Uncle Chayim said, this man could no longer be saved, even by a team of medical specialists.

My aunt continued telling us how furious these Germans had become and how they had demanded that my uncle save their friend. Uncle Chayim was trying to tell them that he was only a veterinarian, who did his best work with animals. He suggested that they take the wounded soldier to a town and have a medical doctor try to do whatever he could, even though he didn't think this soldier could be helped any longer. But the two Germans were shouting and insisting Uncle Chayim must save him – or else he must pay with his life!

The wounded soldier died, and Uncle Chayim was murdered by the two Germans. They shot my uncle in the head.

My uncle's funeral was very sad. The family were all there. Bubbie and Zaida Rosenberg looked so much older at Uncle Chayim's funeral, and I worried about losing them. They had lost someone very precious – a son. All my uncles, aunts, and cousins were weeping for their loss. The other people who attended the funeral cried because they too had lost a dear friend, a good person. While Uncle Chayim was being eulogized and many people made little speeches, saying what my uncle meant to them, I started to wander away. The cemetery in Goray was on a hill outside of town, one of the few places where Jews were still allowed to go. As I wandered away from the crowd, I caught a glimpse of my father's face. He was still not crying. He wasn't talking. He just looked as though he were in agony inside.

I was quite a distance from the funeral crowd, but I could hear the rabbi and the other men's voices, eulogizing my uncle in a low tone. I looked down from the cemetery, and I could see my hometown, Goray, quite clearly. I could see the ghetto area where the Jews lived. I recognized some of my friend's homes. I saw Bubbie and Zaida Rosenberg's house. They lived about a block and a half from our house. I saw the house where I was born and where I still lived. Bubbie and Zaida Daroven's house (Mama's parents) was behind our house. I looked at the houses that my Polish friends used to live in next door to us. I also saw the school I was supposed to start in September of 1939, had there been no war. Now Jewish children were not allowed in school. Only gentiles could attend. I looked and wondered if this town would ever be a free place for me and the others to live in. Would I ever be allowed to learn in that school?

I was nine years old, and I didn't even know the *Abetzadla* (ABCs). My gentile friends had been learning for two and a half years now. Junia and Wanda sometimes sneaked into our house at night, bringing along their notebooks and reading books from school. They read and wrote, subtracted and added, but I just looked at them with great envy. "I am plain ignorant," I thought to myself. All I knew was how to read and write a little Yiddish. My father had organized a class in Yiddish studies for about twenty children. His youngest sister, Sara Deena, was our teacher in the basement of Bubbie and Zaida's house. It was all done in secrecy.

As I looked down from the hill of the cemetery, I wondered what would happen next in my life. I decided that the war would soon end, and we would all live happily ever after.

One afternoon, still early in the war years, my friends Chana and Mayta came over to my house and asked me to come along to Rochele's house so we could play in her backyard. As we were passing the street near our big synagogue, we heard loud laughter and, at the same time, someone crying. We ran toward the sounds, and we saw six Polish men surrounding the rabbi, laughing and hitting him with a rubber hose. The rabbi was begging them to stop, but they just kept on hitting him and slapping him in the face. When the rabbi would fall to the ground, they would pull him up by his beard and prop him up against a wall. One man shouted, "So, you dirty Jew, you were hiding in the synagogue, trying to get away with not having to cut off your beard. We will do it for you now, *parszywy Żyd* [dirty Jew]!" And they continued to beat the rabbi.

Several Jewish men came running over and tried to reason with these hoodlums, asking them to leave the rabbi alone. Then these six big bullies turned their hoses on these men and ordered them to stay indoors. When the Jewish men didn't give up, we heard a shot from a gun. One of these hoodlums shouted, holding a revolver up high, "If all you Jewish men don't disappear immediately, our guns will be aimed at you this time, not in the air. Go home and stay behind closed doors!"

My two friends and I stood there trembling, looking at each other, trying to decide whether to run home or to stay. By now there was a big crowd of Polish Christians watching, so the three of us went unnoticed by the mob.

The rabbi's face was covered with blood. He kept on falling to the ground and passing out. They dragged him over to a water pump. All the people, including Chana, Mayta, and I, followed them. They pumped water on the rabbi's face. When he came to, they ordered him: "Sing, Rabbi, or we will beat you some more!"

The rabbi tried to make some sound by moving his blood-covered lips, but no sound came out. He just stared at these people who had no feelings for humanity – for Jewish humanity. The three of us were hysterical. But we watched.

After another beating, the rabbi of Goray passed out for the last time. Our rabbi was dead. One of these wild men went over and cut off the rabbi's beard as he lay drenched in a pool of his own blood.

When World War II began in Poland on September 1, 1939, I can remember running from the bombs, together with my family. As the Germans were bombing and their fighter planes zoomed over our heads, all of us, Jews and Gentiles, ran toward the forest to hide from our common enemy, the Germans. At age six and a half, I was scared, of course. But we were all in the same situation. We were all Polish citizens running away from a confrontation between Polish and German armies fighting to win.

I remember quite clearly the mobilization in my hometown, Goray. I remember it being a most interesting day. The men who were going off to fight the war were somber. They lined up in the streets. Part of the time they stood at attention; one man in an army uniform spoke to them, and they would salute him. Then they just stood around talking to each other quietly. Here and there one could see a hand waving at the women and children on the other side of town. I stood there holding my mother's hand.

Many years have gone by since then. I now realize what a curious child I was and how I observed what was going on. I remember the gentile women and children standing, wearing gray and white shawls on their shoulders or over their heads when it began to drizzle. They stared at their husbands, sons, and fathers in silence.

The Jewish women, on the other hand, were quite vocal. They spoke loudly to each other and cried tears of sadness. They feared the outcome. They felt Germany would devour these men in no time. "Victory for Poland is not what this war is about," said one Jewish woman, whose son was among the draftees.

There were several men in Polish uniforms making speeches, and the future soldiers applauded them. I didn't understand much of the speeches, nor did I care to. The only words I remember were those ending the speeches: "We will fight to our last drop of blood and the last button on our uniform!"

When the men got on the wagons and the horses started pulling the wagons away from Goray, the Christian women waved and shouted, "Victory for Poland! Victory!" The Jewish mothers and wives were crying a lot. They ran after these wagons and cried out, "Come home soon, alive and well!" "Take care of yourself, son!"

"Don't get killed and leave me a widow and our children orphans," yelled my aunt Hudel, as her husband Mailach's wagon pulled away. She ran after his wagon until it was out of sight. The Jewish wives and mothers were very emotional and very outspoken of their feelings. They said they wanted their men home, alive and well.

Sure enough, only two weeks passed, and it was all over. One evening when my mother answered a knock on our door, there stood a clean-shaven Polish soldier in his uniform. He had clear blue eyes and wore a soldier's envelope-type hat. The buttons on his uniform jacket were all cut off. "Mailach?" asked my mother. "It's really you?"

Suddenly our house came alive. We had our uncle Mailach back home with us! Aunt Hudel and her two little boys, Mechal and Usher, had been living with us for the last two weeks. Uncle Mailach looked good as a soldier, I thought. I just never thought of Uncle Mailach's looks before. He told us that all the men from Goray had come home, except for two. One was killed in action, and the other one was taken prisoner of war by the Germans. The one taken prisoner was Mr. and Mrs. Zlomainsky's son.

The next day German soldiers came marching into Goray, the officers on horses and the soldiers on foot. A sheet of gloom covered the town. My parents and others had that fearful look on their faces. My friends and I went over very close to these soldiers, and we tried to converse with them. "Bring us something to drink," they asked of us, as they sat down on the ground.

We ran to my friend's Yochi's house, next door to Chaya Katz's store. Yochi's mother gave us a pitcher of water, and Chaya Katz called us into her store and gave us a basket filled with lemonade and cherry drinks in bottles. "Here," said Chaya Katz. "Take these over to the soldiers. They must be thirsty," she said. "They are human, even though they are German and big anti-Semites."

The soldiers thanked us very politely. They patted us on our heads and said, "Gute Kinder, schoene Kinder" [good children, pretty children]. My friends and I wondered why the world around us was so scared of this army. Little did we know then how these smiling faces would later turn on us and kill all my friends – and so many more children like my dear friends – only because they were born Jewish.

━━━

It was now March 1944. I felt my life in the kriuvka, as well as in this world, was coming to an end for sure. I was lying under the same dirty hay cover, with my mother on one side of me and Janice on the other side. Josh lay quietly next to Janice, and next to him was our friend Srulki. Josh was wearing one of Marinka Kowalik's dresses, and his hair was long and blonde. With all the dirt in his hair, it looked yellowish. Josh was posing as a girl in case they found us and we tried to pass as gentiles. It was a long shot, but we thought we'd stand a better chance as females. The only circumcised males in Europe at that time were Jewish, so we made this emaciated boy wear a dress. As if we really stood a chance!

As much as we all suffered, I always felt sorry for Josh. Even with just a spot of light here and there, I could see that Josh looked worse than the others. He always looked very worried and very much alone. He did have a strong belief in God, and he had his little book of *Tehillim*, which he read over and over, hoping that God would hear his prayers.

It was still bitter cold in our *kriuvka*. The lack of food and the gruesome conditions under the floors were not only weakening our bodies but were also affecting our minds. There was no water to drink or to wash our hands and faces with, ever. No changing our clothes, ever. I was still wearing the same gray shirt, riddled with lice and other bugs. Hunger, still a daily problem, was now felt somewhat less. Mama gave out the two or three potatoes every evening. We ate in silence, and we continued to wait for the next day, having doubts that there would be a next day. I was less sensitive to life, or even to death, by now. My feelings were getting numb. We lay there and rotted away, day after day, without a shred of hope from the outside world. None of the Kowaliks took time to talk to us anymore. Mrs. Kowalik didn't even threaten us anymore. I felt that she knew we would soon die, and no one would ever know of our existence on her property.

When evening came, I automatically crawled up on my hands and knees through the short straw tunnel at the sound of the first knock on the boards. I would take the pot of potatoes. We ate the potatoes, most of the time while lying under the cover, without making a sound. And then we would lie there some more. When we heard dogs barking in the distance, I no longer held my breath, thinking they were leading the Germans or the Poles to find Jews in hiding and drag them out to their deaths. It almost didn't matter any longer. Even when I heard dogs louder and closer to us, I no longer had that crucial panic I once had, and that fervent desire to live. Sometimes, when a fox used to sneak into the courtyard and eat a chicken, all the animals would react in an uproar and become loud and frightened. We would also panic, thinking that the bad people were searching for us to destroy us, to end our existence. Now, we were no longer as jumpy as before. I felt that death could not be much worse than this existence, with no end in sight. Slowly March 1944 was ending, and it was the beginning of April 1944.

Lantern in hand, stern-looking Maria Kowalik paid us a visit one evening in April 1944. She leaned to one side in our hiding place as she began to talk to us, mainly to my mother. She told Mama that last Sunday Mr. Zlomainsky had talked to her in church. He told her that Hitler's army had gone as far as Stalingrad. Around Stalingrad, the Germans were taking a terrible beating just by being so far into the Russian territory, and they couldn't endure its harsh, cold weather. Zlomainsky said that the German soldiers were dying by the score. "They are falling like flies," he said. Zlomainsky told her that this was a very important turning point in this horrible war. He thought that from now on, the Germans could only retreat and go back all the way, until they either gave up or were completely destroyed.

"What else did Mr. Zlomainsky tell you?" asked my mother eagerly.

"He said you should try to hang on to life. You may stand a

chance and survive one day soon," answered Maria. Holding up her lantern as she got ready to leave, she looked at all of us and whispered quietly, "I hope Zlomainsky is right." Then she turned around and left us.

Mr. Zlomainsky kept sending more encouraging messages with Mrs. Kowalik during the month of April. The messages were, "Hang on. There is hope for you. You might be freed soon." Once he told Maria, "The Jews may make it all the way to America!"

Hope was being rekindled in our aching hearts. We began to wait impatiently for more good news from Mr. Zlomainsky. He was our only link to the real world outside our *kriuvka*. Hope! Yes, hope was once again budding inside us as we were lying weakly under the cover and time was passing slowly.

One day at the end of April 1944, Maria Kowalik informed us that she had confided in Mr. and Mrs. Chaika, her daughter Wlatka's in-laws, about her hiding out Srulki, and she had told them what a good tailor Srulki was. Now the Chaikas would like to "borrow" Srulki, hide him in their storage room, and have him make some pants and jackets for their family. For Srulki, it was certainly a break to go from our *kriuvka* to a roomy storage room where he could stand and sit on a chair like a normal person. A palace compared to our hideout! He would probably be fed better, too. We were sad to see him leave. Our good-byes were very emotional. "Who knows if we'll ever see each other again in this world?" cried Mama.

The month of May was a very turbulent month. There was evidence that the Germans were actually retreating. As in the beginning of the war in 1939 when they had bombed to conquer land, they were now bombing cities, towns, and villages to destroy everything they possibly could as they were leaving. The difference for us was that in 1939 we all ran together from the bombs – Jews and gentiles alike. We were all Polish citizens at the time. Now we Jews were in hiding, and Zlomainsky's message was that most of the bombing occurred during the night. So now we stayed up nights. Now it was the four of us, without Srulki, whom we missed very much.

We gathered every night right near the two boards that opened. We now heard airplanes zooming over Lada, and we actually began hearing bombing in the distance. As more days and nights went by, more and more bombings were heard. The sounds of the bombings were getting closer all the time. One night Mama went out into the courtyard after the sounds of the planes and bombing subsided, and she said she could actually see some flames and lots of smoke from another village. So night after night we sat curled up near our exit in case Lada would be bombed. At dawn we'd return to our nest, crawl under the cover, and fall asleep.

Sound asleep at daybreak near the end of May 1944, I thought I was dreaming when I heard my mother's voice in my ears: "Naomi, get up! Josh, wake up! The bombs are falling on us!"

I just lay there, trying to continue my dream. Mama and Janice started dragging me and Josh, and as Mama was pulling me by my hair, I began to realize that it was not a dream. In fact, it was a nightmare in real life. The loudness of the bombs falling made it quite real to me now. So with all my might, I started to crawl on my own. When we reached the boards, they were on fire, and I started backing away. But Mama and Janice pushed the burning boards with all their strength.

When the two boards fell to the ground away from the tunnel, I couldn't believe the sight before my eyes. The barns and stables were burning, and the animals were running and falling on top of each other as they were burning, making awful, loud sounds. Bales of straw were falling from the lofts and rolling on the ground in full flame.

"Let's go, kids!" yelled my mother as she jumped into the fiery yard. I tried to jump, but I couldn't. My legs wouldn't get straight. Janice jumped out quickly after Mama. Josh and I had not realized that we could not walk. Through two long, harsh winters in hiding, we always curled up in a fetal position to try to keep warm. Since we were of growing age, the muscles in the backs of our knees had grown together. So Mama and Janice grabbed us and pulled us down to the ground. Of course, we bruised ourselves, but there was no time to complain. Josh and I started crawling on our hands and knees after Mama and Janice, who led the way. Crawling between the animals and other obstacles, we made it out of the courtyard.

What was going on was unbelievable! Beams were falling, flames rising, animals screeching from pain, and people's voices in the distance, yelling at each other to run. Now the grass we were crawling on was on fire, and we must escape all this. "Impossible!" I thought.

Mama and Janice were running. Josh and I were crawling fast, but we just couldn't keep up with them. We continued to follow Mama and Janice, who were now ahead of us. We began to feel wet grass under us, then muddy grass under our hands and knees as we began to get into a swamp. Josh and I started crying, screaming, and begging Mama and Janice to slow down and to please keep us from dying in the mud. They turned around and came back to us. Janice picked up Josh and carried him around her neck. Mama carried me, like a three-year-old child, my arms around her neck and my head on her shoulder. I'm not sure how long all this took, but by that time we were deep into the swamp, and Mama and Janice managed to put Josh and me down on a tree branch.

The sun was shining brightly, and all we could see were bushes and wild tall grass and trees growing out of the mud. Mama and Janice leaned against tree trunks as if they were sitting. We were out in the wilderness, in a swamp, with all kinds of creatures in it!

We were now silent. Bewildered, out of breath, I was clinging to the tree branch in the swamp, still in shock over how we managed to escape the burning bombs. Trying to breathe normally, I wanted to ask Mama, "What now?" But I didn't dare say anything. I knew her answer would be "I don't know."

Mama looked at Josh and me and she said, "If I hadn't pulled you two by your hair, you would have burnt to death!"

"Well, you should have left me there to die in my sleep! It would have been over for me, and I wouldn't have to die once more. How many times do I have to die? You did me no favor bringing me out here to die in the mud!" I yelled at my best friend. My Mama, my "Minnak." I was crying and crying and really letting go.

It was catching, it seemed. For now Janice and Josh were also crying and letting go. Mama just sat there, her face full of pain, not answering anything. As I calmed down, I began to feel guilty for blaming my mother for having saved my life from the fiery bombs. I didn't know quite how to make it up to her, so I just kept quiet.

After awhile, Mama started moving around, looking here and there. She noticed some small logs in the swamp, and she took me, then Josh, and put us on top of the logs. Mama and Janice began to feel the mud oozing up as they too sat on the logs, which were now beginning to sink. The day was over. As night fell, it got very cold. Mama climbed up a small tree, and she saw heavy smoke and some flames still burning in the distance. Mama declared that we had better do something to try to survive. She told Josh and me that she and Janice would get out of the swamp and see if they could find a place for us to save ourselves. "We have come so far in our struggle. Now is not a good time to give up. The Germans are obviously retreating. Maybe we can make it. Maybe we can outlast them after all!"

"No! We can't let them go," yelled Josh in his squeaky voice. "They will never come back for us," he continued. "They will find a place for themselves and leave us here to die." I could feel his body trembling as he was talking and leaning against me. I agreed not to let Mama and Janice go.

Another day passed. Still no food, and nothing to drink. We just sat and waited. On the third day, our skin began to form green bubbles. They were blisters filled with pus, infected by the swamp. By late afternoon our bodies and our faces had blotches filled with the green stuff. We were tired, and we were very weak.

"Come, Mama," said Janice that evening. "Let us not give in to death. Let us not listen to the two little ones. If we do, we are all going to die a slow death out here in the swamp. We have to go out and find a place to hide and get something to eat. Mama, you and I know that we will never leave them here to die. We will return." She said this turning to Josh and me. "Let us go, Mama, and prove it to them."

Mama and Janice held hands as they started out of the swamp and left us alone in the night. Josh and I didn't talk, but I'm sure our thoughts were very much the same. Many terrifying hours passed in the dark. Josh and I leaned against one another. The swampy, muddy water was all over our bodies by now. We could barely keep our heads and shoulders out of the swamp. "They really left us to die and be eaten by horrible creatures in the swamp!" I said. Josh didn't answer. He was dozing as he leaned against me. I was very sad and very scared.

Suddenly – a splash in the water! I heard a voice. "Mama, where are you?" It was my sister's voice! Mama had fallen into a deep area, and she dropped the half-loaf of bread she was carrying for us. "Here, Janice. Here!" answered Mama. Janice picked up Mama and found the bread soaked in mud. "Eat, children, eat!" said Mama.

We forced some of this soaked bread down our throats, and then I asked, "Did you find a place for us to hide?"

"Tell them, Janice," said Mama, "while I get this mud out of my ears, nose, and hair."

Janice was excited. Her voice was upbeat. "I'll tell it to you as fast as I can," she said. "Mama and I couldn't believe our eyes when we saw Mrs. Kowalik's house on the hill, still standing! Out of 120 houses that Lada had, only 2 weren't destroyed, and 1 was the Kowaliks'! All her barns and stables were gone, and all her animals had burned to death. Maria Kowalik had been sure that we had all died, together with her animals. As a matter of fact, when Maria saw us, she crossed herself and yelled out, 'Jesus Christus, are you ghosts? Am I seeing things?' But we assured her that we were all alive," continued Janice.

"Maria told us that Mr. Zlomainsky had come out and asked about us, but she told him that we had all died. Zlomainsky was sad and said, 'What a pity!' He thinks the Russians will be occupying our area within weeks. He was upset that all the suffering we went through was in vain. 'What a shame,' he told Maria. But now that we are alive, she has no place for us, she said. 'What about your attic?' asked Mama in desperation. Her attic, she told us, is a dangerous place. Any move can be heard in the house. And people are constantly coming and going in her house. So Mama promised Mrs. Kowalik that all day long we will lie there covered with straw and not make a move. Mama assured her that we are used to lying still without making a move or a sound. Finally, she agreed to take us in. So let us go before she changes her mind," concluded Janice.

Mama and Janice helped Josh and me by carrying us out of the swamp. When they became very tired, they dragged us by our arms. When we reached dry land in the field, Josh and I crawled on our own. I was out of breath now, but there was no time to rest. It was important to reach Mrs. Kowalik before she fell asleep waiting for us.

It was quite a distance from the swamp to the Kowaliks' house. Running for life from the fire bombs, I didn't realize how far it was. As we got near the house, I saw how all the buildings were gone. It had all turned to ashes and debris, including our *kriuvka* with that horrible hay cover. In a way, I was secretly glad that our sub-human – even subanimal – nest was gone, even though I had no idea what would come next.

Maria Kowalik was the only one up waiting for us. She showed us the ladder to the attic and told us that she had already prepared a hole in the straw, up in the attic, close to the edge of the gable roof, where it met the outside wall. She gave Josh and me a cup of milk to drink before we made it up to the attic. Maria lifted her lantern and pointed toward our new hole in the straw. We got inside it very fast. We just slid down the smooth straw. (Straw is yellow and smooth, unless you hit an edge – then you cut yourself. Hay is crunchy and warmer, but very itchy.)

Maria was on the mound of straw with her lantern in hand. She looked down at us and said, "Here I am doing this again. Putting up Jews in my own house, in my own attic, when I know that any time, any tall German who walks into my house can push the trap-door to this attic open with one hand, climb up, and find you here. Why am I risking my seven children's lives as well as my own? I just don't understand myself. Do you understand me, Faiga? If you do, tell me. Tell me why!"

My mother stood on her knees and touched Mrs. Kowalik's hand. "Maria, it's very easy to see why," said Mama. "Your heart is in the right place. You know you are doing the most noble, most humane thing a person can do for others. You are saving lives, especially innocent children's lives. God will reward you in many ways. You will see. I promise you. Also, when Saverek Zlomainsky finds out that we are still alive, and that we may survive this war thanks to you, I'm quite sure he will help you in many ways. He's a very good and smart person, too. He also knows that when you save lives, it's as if you are saving the world. So please, tomorrow get in touch with him," pleaded Mama.

"I certainly will go to see him tomorrow," said Maria. "All I have left now is this house and whatever is growing in the field. Come harvest time, I won't even have anywhere to store the crops. All my animals are gone except for a few horses that escaped the bombing."

"God in Heaven will help you, Maria. You will see. You are a good human being, and I'm glad to have you as a friend," said Mama.

Maria put several bales of straw up near us to make sure we could not be seen from any angle. Then she climbed down the ladder and went to her bed.

In the next few days, the green pus sores began to dry somewhat. They were healing, and that gave me something to do. I remember poking holes in the healing sores with a firm straw helping the pus to run out, and wiping off the pus with my gray dirty shirt that I was still wearing. Then the sores would become dry. The next day or so, I became busy peeling off the skin bit by bit. I was so busy with my sores day and night that I forgot to worry or to be frightened. I just made myself forget who I was and that I was not allowed to live in this world. I just pretended to be a monkey in a cage, picking and eating my own skin as if it were a delicacy. But at the same time, a glimpse of who I really was would remind me to hate myself for having become this animal.

Other things also happened in the next few days in the attic. Mrs. Kowalik must have had a mental block about our bodily functions. Mama was scared to remind her of it, so as not to become too much trouble. So Mama quietly looked around the attic and found a large clay pot for us to use. Since we almost never drank, and we ate very little, Mama figured the pot would last us a week or so. Mama decided that when it got close to full, Janice would climb down somehow, while the Kowaliks were out in the field working. Janice would then open the door to the outside, look around, and when she felt it was safe, she would empty the pot in the grass and return with the empty pot. That was Mama's plan.

About four days after settling in the attic, in the middle of the night, we heard a loud bang, as if something broke. We all popped our heads up and listened. "Jesus Christus!" we heard Juzefka crying out. "I'm all wet, and it smells terrible! It comes from the Żydy upstairs. The whole mass is coming from them. They ruined my bed! Get them out of here!"

That was when we realized that the clay pot had burst and spilled through the ceiling. Juzefka's bed was directly under that pot. Poor Juzefka had to take all this from Jews! Finally, Maria provided us with an iron pot.

After Maria saw Zlomainsky, she came up to the attic and told us that when Zlomainsky found out about us and that we were tucked away in her attic, he was overjoyed. But Maria Kowalik complained. Had the Jews been found in the barn by Germans, she told Zlomainsky, she still might have been able to deny having known about us. But in her attic, there was no denying. Zlomainsky told Maria that the Germans were so busy now in their retreat, trying to destroy the world they thought would always belong to them and fighting off the Russian army, that it was unlikely they would find out about the Rosenbergs in her attic. Of course, he told her, if they knew of Jews hiding out, the confrontation with the Russians wouldn't keep them from going first after the Jews; therefore, he emphasized, she had to be very discreet about keeping the Jews a little longer. She also complained to Zlomainsky about her situation come harvest time. Zlomainsky looked her straight in the eyes and assured her, she told us, that in a few days, he would personally be involved in rebuilding her barns and stables. He promised to do much to help her put her farm back in place. Maria just couldn't believe what she heard from Mr. Zlomainsky. We were also stunned that this great man could do so much for her in order to help us survive.

"Unbelievable!" said Mama, after Maria left the attic. "Saverek Zlomainsky must be an angel sent from heaven," said Mama.

"So where are these Russians, our liberators?" I asked.

"And why are the Germans still here, after they bombed and destroyed so much?" asked Josh.

Mama turned to us and said, "War isn't a simple game. It takes a lot to destroy a power like Hitler and his armies."

Mama started telling us stories about World War I, when she was only eleven years old. She told us about the Cossacks, who used to come to town and make a pogrom against the Jews. They would terrorize the Jewish community. They would rob and beat up some Jews, take away their valuable possessions, and then leave. She said she was afraid of the Russians then. The Cossacks were really terrors. But next to the so-called cultured Germans, they were angels.

"The Germans have destroyed our nation without any reason whatsoever. We were not at war with Germany or any other nation. We just wanted to live peacefully with all nations. Maybe if we had had our own country, this wouldn't have happened," Mama went on. "We have been persecuted for thousands of years, since the destruction of our Holy Land. Who will the world persecute next, now that the Jews are murdered?"

We continued to wait in Mrs. Kowalik's attic. But now we waited with hope of good things to come.

Mr. Zlomainsky kept his promise. Big wagonloads of lumber started to arrive at the Kowalik property. Sacks filled with grain, hardware such as nails, hammers, and other stuff – even live chickens in crates came to Maria's house. Mrs. Kowalik's elongated face started looking somewhat rounder to me. Needless to say, everyone was happier. For the next six weeks, we could hear the Kowalik brothers, sisters, and friends hammering away all day long, building new barns and new stables. I remember watching them through a small opening, which I made by moving away a shingle on the roof.

What remains in my mind even today, though, was not so much seeing the walls going up, the rafters put in place, the gates being put together. What I remember, of all things, was seeing Yanek drinking water from a pitcher, and the water running down on his bare chest. I licked my lips, and I could feel the cold water. I was drooling from thirst, and I felt faint. If only we could have a pitcher with water to drink! Six long weeks in this attic, surrounded with straw, and all day the hot summer sun was beating down on the roof above us. If only the Russian army would come marching in and make us free to go outside. We didn't sleep much – it was too hot. But we could not move around much and remind them of our presence. So we just lay there in silence.

On July 27, 1944, at about 6:00 A.M., lightening-striking, thunderous-sounding, earthshaking sounds awakened us. The whole house shook. Seconds later another wave of the same deafening bangs was moving the world around us. As we four jumped up, we heard Mrs. Kowalik yelling to her children to get out of the house. As she threw up the ladder to our trapdoor opening, she screamed out to us, "Jews, you are on your own!"

Somehow we made it down the ladder and out of the house. At first we all crawled around outside, not knowing what to do, hiding in the bushes. Then Mama yelled out, "Hurry, children, hurry! We are in the middle of a war front between the Germans and the Russians!"

Again, Josh and I were on our hands and knees, crawling as fast as we could. We saw people running very fast. There was so much commotion all around us that they didn't even notice us. I was so bewildered – I had no idea that there was going to be a war front right here. What was a war front, anyway?

We were now in the garden. I saw lots of red, beautiful strawberries growing on the ground near me. I couldn't believe my eyes – strawberries! I picked one and put it in my mouth. "Heaven!" I thought. "I must be in strawberry heaven!" So I picked them and ate them nonstop. For about two minutes, I was ecstatic. I was outside, under the blue sky, eating strawberries!

But Mama, who must have been ahead, turned around and came over to me, with a smear of red strawberry near her lips. She grabbed me by my hand and warned me, "No more picking strawberries today if you want to live!"

I followed my mother out of the garden. Now we found ourselves in the open field. We saw people on horses, galloping at maximum speed; people on wagons, riding fast; and people running as fast as humanly possible. "They are all aiming for the forest!" Mama shouted in order to be heard.

We felt very vulnerable and exposed out in the open field. We were not sure what was the least dangerous route for us to take. There was so little time to think and make a major decision! Mama knew that if we made it into the forest, the gentiles would kill us for sure. If we stayed out in the field, there were jeeps filled with Germans – some now coming off the road and some riding the opposite way toward the road – who would surely shoot us. There was not much choice for us at this crucial turning point!

Mama decided that we just had to keep moving around in the field and look busy. As we got further out in the field, we heard – in between the Russians' Katyusha rockets and other ammunition sounds – someone calling our name: "Rosenbergs! Rosenbergs!"

It was Yanek Kowalik, and he was pointing to the ground. His other words sounded like "Get in! Get in the cellar!" Then he ran away toward the forest.

Huffing and puffing, we arrived where Yanek Kowalik had been, and there were two wooden doors on the ground and several bales of hay on each side of them. One door was open. "It's a cellar! A field cellar!" shouted Mama. "Let's get in – quickly!"

There was actually a stairway going down. The cellar was half filled with potatoes. We all flopped down on the potatoes except Mama. She closed the doors and remained on the steps, trying to hear or see what was really going on – what was happening out there. Some light came in between the two doors. We didn't know how safe we were there, since they were doors that anyone could open, but at least we were out of the open field.

The fighting out there continued. The shooting sounds – and now, more often, the Katyusha sounds – made the stone walls of the cellar feel like they were moving. Mama kept opening the door just slightly once in awhile. She told us what she saw from a distance. She saw Germans in vehicles and on motorcycles coming and going all the time.

After about an hour, Mama saw no more people from the local villages. She seemed excited, but she was trembling as she spoke to us. She couldn't get over it – so much was going on out there! But Mama was scared. I crawled up to her once in awhile. I touched her, but she ordered me to go down and find a corner to lean on back in the cellar and told me to behave. She was extremely eager to see the outside.

The next few hours were nerve-wracking to us. At about three or four in the afternoon, things became quieter. Now we heard shooting sporadically. Late in the afternoon, we heard a motorcycle riding right over the two slightly slanted doors to our cellar. Mama lifted the door a bit and saw a German soldier zooming away on his bike and throwing a hand grenade to his right. We heard the explosion, but we didn't know if anyone got hurt. "He's desperate," said Mama. But our hearts turned over from fear at the thought that a German soldier was so close to us.

Finally, in the evening, it became quiet. We each settled into a corner of the cellar on top of the potatoes. I was in the sort of middle corner, across from the stairway, where Mama decided to continue to stay. I was leaning against the rough stones of the cellar wall and keeping an eye on Mama.

"All these potatoes in this cellar. Why didn't she ever think of giving us a few more, so we wouldn't starve?" said my sister.

We all sat in silence. We waited and waited, hoping to hear good news. A knock on the doors got our adrenaline flowing.

"It's Juza," came the voice from outside. Juzefka opened the cellar door, the pot of potatoes in her hands. Mama was right there to take it from her.

"Juzefka," said Mama excitedly, "Tell us the good news! Tell us about the Russians. They are here, aren't they?" asked Mama eagerly.

"There are no Russians," answered Juzefka. "There are no Russians here."

"But the front," said Mama, "all day long there was a war front in this area. The Katyushas, the Germans running away desperately, that was a front!" insisted Mama.

"You would think so, wouldn't you?" answered Juzefka. "It was only a clash between the Partisans and some German soldiers. Your eager anticipation was all in vain. All in vain," repeated Juzefka. And she closed the door as she was leaving. She also closed all hope that was in our hearts.

Sadly, we all gathered around Mama on the stairs. The pot with the boiled potatoes was standing right there on a step. None of us thought of hunger now. We were filled with despair and sadness. I put my head on Mama's lap and cried quietly.

Mama touched my head, her hand still trembling. She said, "I just don't believe what Juzefka said. She doesn't know much. The village people don't know politics. All day, today, was a confrontation between armies with heavy artillery. It was no skirmish or clash between Partisans and Germans. Partisans don't have Katyushas. Oh, how I wish I could talk to Mr. Zlomainsky! He is intelligent and knowledgeable, and he surely knows what happened today!"

Mama gave out the potatoes and told us to eat. She said she was hopeful that we would soon be free, and we needed our strength to wait a little longer. After we ate, Mama asked us to go back to our corners while she remained on top of the steps, close to the two doors. Sitting in the dark, Juzefka's words came back to haunt me: "No Russians are here.... only a clash with the Partisans ... Your suffering was in vain, in vain." I became sad and depressed. Hope vanished again! And so we sat for hours and hours of the night, until eventually we all fell asleep.

At dawn, I heard a knock on the door upstairs. I didn't even bother to pick up my head. I just wanted to sleep forever. As I was still half asleep, I heard someone open the door. None of us was moving. We were like heavy stones.

I heard a voice saying, "*Stara* [old woman], wake up!" (Mama was forty-one years old now. Maria was about ten years older than

135

Mama, but she still called her "old woman"!) I lifted my head, and I saw Maria pulling my mother by her hair, trying to wake her up. "The Russians are here! Can you hear me? You made it! You are free to live!"

Mama looked straight into Maria's eyes. Janice, Josh, and I all stared at the top of the stairs. We looked at each other without moving. I was convinced that I was having a wishful dream, so I lowered my head and closed my eyes. But Maria Kowalik kept on talking.

"You have been waiting for this day for a very long time," she said. I still didn't hear Mama making a sound. "Faiga, say something!" Maria was now shaking my mother.

"How – how do you know that the Russians are here? Really here?" Mama managed to ask.

"How do I know?" said Maria. "They are in my house, eating up all I have! They are a bunch of pigs! But they are the liberators – right, Faiga?"

"Can I go to your house and see Russian soldiers for myself?" asked Mama.

"They are moving out soon. Perhaps when the next group comes you'll be able to see them for yourself. I don't know how far away the Germans have retreated. I'll come back later today and bring you news of the latest happenings," said Maria as she was leaving and closing the cellar door behind her.

Sitting in the corner not moving, I felt a surge of guilt go through me. My daddy, murdered. Chaya-Leeba taken to Majdanek concentration camp, never to return alive. Perele, shot and buried alive in a mass grave. My grandparents from both sides, sent to camps. Uncles, aunts, cousins, all dead. My friends, my dear friends, all sent to their death in the camps. How could it be that I was alive? That the four of us were alive?

"You made it! You are free to live!" Those were the words Mrs. Kowalik said to us just minutes ago. Didn't we owe it to the rest of them to be dead?

Then a voice inside me said, "I must live on. We must live on. We must live and always remember the others and tell about them. We must live on – for us and for them. And always remind the people in the world what we witnessed!"

Finally my mother came down off the stairs. We started to move and crawl toward each other. We met in the middle of the cellar on the hard, cold potatoes. We put our arms around each other's necks, and we hugged and cried for a very long time. We were stunned and filled with mixed emotions. Were we really free to live?

At about 10:00 A.M., Yanek showed up in the potato cellar. "We are free, Yanek, and I want to thank you. You showed us this cellar when we needed a place to escape," said Mama.

"I'm not sure you are free," responded Yanek.

"Why do you say that? Aren't the Russians here?" asked Mama.

"Oh, yes, they are here. A bunch of soldiers stopped me on the road this morning and frisked me, then followed me home. They are in our house right now, drinking and singing." Yanek seemed a bit sad.

"I heard rumors," said Yanek, "that Stalin gave orders to kill any Jew who managed to survive Europe under Germany's occupation."

"Don't be silly, Yanek. It can't possibly be true." Mama actually laughed when she said that.

"Did you say that there are Russian soldiers in your house right now?" asked Mama.

"Yes," answered Yanek.

"I would very much like to go with you, Yanek, and see them for myself," said my mother.

"They will kill you, Mrs. Rosenberg. Remember, you are Jewish," answered Yanek.

"How can I forget?" chuckled Mama. "So, I won't tell them about being Jewish," insisted Mama.

Yanek grinned with pity in his eyes as he looked us over. "You look like a dead Jew who came out of the grave to find out what's new," said Yanek.

Mama was really trying hard to go with Yanek. "Look, Yanek, I still don't have horns, do I? Take me with you, sir!" Mama reached out to Yanek. He hesitated for a moment, then took Mama by her hand, and they started out the door. My mother stopped. She turned to us, her children, and she warned us to be very quiet in the cellar. "I'll be back soon, with good news, I hope," said Mama as she closed the two cellar doors.

It was many hours before Mama came back. We were frantically worried. Upon her return, Mama seemed excited. We all crawled over to her to hear every word she was trying to tell us, hoping it was good news. And Mama told us everything she experienced in the outside world that day.

When she first saw Russian soldiers, her heart was racing with excitement. Healthy-looking men. Our liberators! She said she felt like kissing their feet. The first question Mama asked these soldiers was, "Are there Jews in Russia?"

"Of course, there are Jews in our Motherland Russia," answered one soldier.

She asked whether Stalin accepted Jews as Russian citizens.

"By us, all is *f'sho roovno* [we are all equal]!" answered another healthy-looking soldier.

The soldiers and their superior stared at Mama. The superior asked Mama if, by any chance, she could be a Jewish survivor of the Jewish slaughter by the Nazis? Mama quickly told them that she wasn't Jewish. Then they wanted to know why she was asking so much about Jews. And why did she look like a corpse, so yellow and emaciated, as if she hadn't eaten or seen the light for years? Mama told them that she had a terminal illness and the reason for her inquiries about Jews was because she used to work for Jewish people for many years and now they were all wiped out around here. She told them she liked Jews and would like to see a Russian soldier, if it were possible, who was a Jew. The man in charge took my mother's hand and said to her, "Come with me to the town of Goray, only a few miles from here. There is a Captain Kanievsky there, who is Jewish. I have a feeling he will welcome you."

He walked Mama to his jeep, and Mama tried not to show him how excited she really was. Mama told us that when she arrived in Goray, she tried not to look at anything. It was too painful to see Goray without our loved ones. The Russian in uniform drove her straight to where Captain Kanievsky was. When Mama was face to face with the captain, she asked him one word in Hebrew, "Amcha?" [Are you Jewish?] (Literally translated, it means "What is your nationality?" *Amcha*, I later learned, was a word that Jews in concentration camps used to identify each other.)

No reply was necessary. His eyes filled with tears as he kept staring at my mother. He hugged Mama, and they both cried. He told Mama that she was the first Jewish survivor he had seen so far in Poland. He offered Mama food. He told her that he would help smuggle her through to Russia, where she'd be safe. "The war is still raging not far from us," he told her.

Mama thanked him. Then she told him about her three young children, still in hiding. He became more emotional when he heard about us being alive too. "More tears came running down his pleasant face," Mama told us.

My mother told us how she had managed to hold herself together and had asked Captain Kanievsky many questions. Only he kept on asking my mother how she and her three children had survived all the atrocities. "It's a long story, sir, and you still have Germans to fight right now," Mama told him.

During their conversation, Captain Kanievsky opened up his army bag at one point and pulled out his *tefillin* (phylacteries). "I became lightheaded," said Mama, "remembering how your father used to put on *tefillin* every weekday in the morning to pray to God. But God did not hear his prayers," said Mama, momentarily bitter toward God. Captain Kanievsky told her that he had promised his own mother that whenever possible he would put on his *tefillin* and pray.

The captain told my mother to stay hidden a little longer, until the Germans were completely pushed back. Then he told my mother she should take her three children and go to Russia, where everyone was equal and free. We listened to Mama talk and still felt that we were in a dream. Were we really free? Free to live?

Mr. Zlomainsky quickly got in touch with Maria Kowalik and ordered her to keep us in her attic until he could organize a safe place for us. He was convinced that if we would appear right now, in the middle of all the chaos going on – the Germans just out of sight, and the Russians not stationing the same soldiers for more than a day – the Polish gentiles would go wild, seeing that Jews had survived the Germans. They would surely kill us. So we were back in the attic, only this time we were filled with hope and excitement. And with a lot of mixed emotions, we waited to hear from Mr. Saverek Zlomainsky.

Three weeks later, Zlomainsky sent a driver with a wagon pulled by two horses to pick us up and bring us to his house. We said our good-byes to the Kowaliks. I remember feeling so mixed-up inside. I was both happy and sad. I was angry and grateful at the same time. My comprehension of that day was not very real. It was the first time in my recollection that I only thought of today – right now, as if there would not be a tomorrow – but I wasn't worried.

Riding in the wagon on the road to Mr. Zlomainsky's house, Mama asked the driver to stop over at the Jewish cemetery in Goray. At the cemetery, Mama and Janice helped Josh and me out of the wagon. Josh and I crawled on our hands and knees. We looked around and saw that some of the monuments had been removed and made into a walk. Others were just knocked over. Many looked like they had been crushed by bombs from the battle between the Russians and the Germans as the Germans retreated.

I thought of the time in the forest when Mama wanted us to give ourselves up to be killed and be buried here, in this cemetery in Goray. My heart started racing, and I wanted to run. Then I heard Mama calling us over to where she was standing. "Look, children," said Mama, "from this mountainous cemetery, we can actually see most of Goray."

I looked down, and I felt sick. It just didn't look like my hometown any longer. I felt as if I were actually walking on my own grave. I was relieved to hear Mama say, "Let's go."

Zlomainsky was waiting for us at his house. As we each climbed out of the wagon, he hugged us and asked us to enter his house. When he hugged my mother, they both started to cry. "I can't believe that we are actually alive today, Mr. Zlomainsky," said Mama, "and it's mainly thanks to you, sir."

"Well," said Zlomainsky, "I'm not too sure I can call you 'alive,' the way you all look. But now there is hope for you," he concluded.

Mrs. Zlomainsky brought over four cups of milk and some bread spread with butter. She urged us to eat and drink. There was a lump inside my throat that prevented me from being able to swallow the bread, even though my eyes were staring at this feast of bread, butter, and milk. It had been a long time since my eyes had seen food such as this. I just couldn't believe that we were really in a house, legally invited by wonderful Mr. and Mrs. Zlomainsky. I kept staring upward through their window to the beautiful blue sky. As I looked up, a fearful thought suddenly went through my mind. "What if this is only a dream? What if I wake up and find we are still really inside the *kriuvka*? And what if we . . ."

"Hey, little blonde with the big gray eyes!" called out Mr. Zlomainsky.

"You have to get back on the wagon now. You will all travel to Bilgoray, where I've made arrangements for you and some others who have survived from Goray, Frampol, and Bilgoray. You will share this big barn together, and Russian soldiers will guard you for now."

"Why do we have to be guarded by soldiers?" I asked. The thought of seeing men in uniform frightened me.

"You have to be guarded, or our Polish people might still try to kill you," he answered me sadly, putting his hand on my dirty hair.

"How long do we have to be guarded?" asked Janice.

"Until the Germans are very far from here, and until you find a fairly safe home you can call your own," he replied.

"Mr. Zlomainsky," said my mother, "do you think that we can ride into the center streets of Goray, where we used to live, and see what it's like?" inquired Mama. "Sure, Faiga, just don't linger there," he answered.

We stood in the center of the Goray marketplace, Josh and I on our knees, holding onto Mama's hands. Janice was pacing up and down the street and saying, "Oh, God, oh, God, this is not the town I remember! This is not Goray, where we were born and raised. This is a ghost town, and I feel like I'm going out of my mind here!"

To see the ruins of this town, and the absence of our dear relatives and friends, was devastating. Our minds couldn't deal with it. Where were my grandparents? My cousins, uncles, and aunts? And where were the dear and happy, laughing faces of my friends? Why were they all slaughtered? I'd never see them again. I'd never hear them laughing. How could that be?

Reality was setting in, and I didn't like what I saw. So I closed my eyes and turned my thoughts back several years to the good old days. Now I could see all the people I knew then. Uncles, aunts, cousins who were also my friends, and yes, my two grandmothers and two grandfathers, whom I now missed so much. I could hear their voices ringing in my ears. I could see Bubbie Shaindel handing me several *groshen* and telling me to go buy myself some ice cream. Then she would pat me on my head and tell me what a good girl I was. Zaida Aaron Yankel was smiling, looking at me with pleasure in his eyes, handing me some good fruit he just brought home from the village of Lada. I could see Zaida Yossel and Bubbie Hena fussing over me and my friends on a Sabbath afternoon when I visited them. Bubbie and Zaida's hands were filled with cookies, candy, nuts, and lemonade to drink.

My thoughts took me back now to a normal Friday night in our house. All seven of us standing around the dining table, which was set with a white tablecloth and the two *challah* breads covered with a pretty cloth embroidered by my oldest sister, Chaya-Leeba. A silver candelabra with seven candles lit by my mother is sparkling. The silver *becher* (Kiddush cup), filled with wine, is lifted by my father. Daddy is chanting the Kiddush in his clear, strong voice. We are all looking at him and listening to the Kiddush, which starts with these words, "Va'yehi Erev, Va'yehi Boker . . ." [There was evening and there was morning. On the sixth day of the week, the heavens and the earth and everything on the earth were created by the Lord. Now it is the beginning of the Sabbath.]

Oh, yes, we were one beautiful, shining menorah, as my father used to refer to us, since we were a family of seven. The aroma of my mother's cooking all the good food for the Sabbath was filling my nostrils. I could almost taste the festive meal that followed Daddy's chanting of the Kiddush. I looked forward to Friday nights when we were all dressed in our pretty clothes for the Sabbath. We had all kinds of discussions at the table on Friday nights. My dad would bring us up to date on current events – what he read in the newspapers and what other people told him in the course of the week. He asked each of us how we spent this last week. Did we do any mitzvahs (good deeds) toward others? Did we show respect to our elders? And did we have fun? Daddy would tell us some funny stories and make us all laugh. The laughter was ringing in my ears as my mother tugged at my shoulder, saying, "Naomi, Naomi, get back on the wagon! Why are you always dreaming while you are awake?"

I opened my eyes, and all I saw was this strange place. A strange world all around me. A world I didn't like. Janice was right. This was not the same hometown that we once knew and lived in. I sat in the wagon, and I never looked back. As we rode out of Goray, I turned to my mother and said, "Mama, I never want to see this town again!" Mama put her arm around me and squeezed me tight and close to her.

Mr. Zlomainsky had picked Bilgoray because it was a fairly large city. The Russians had a station in Bilgoray with Russian soldiers coming and going there all the time; therefore, he felt it was the safest place for us to be just then.

In the barn, guarded by Russian soldiers, we came together, thirty-one Jewish people from the towns of Goray, Frampol, and Bilgoray. We were the survivors from about eight thousand people.

Mama was the only person who managed to survive with children. There were two or three who had a sister or brother. All the others were singles with no next of kin.

At first we didn't know most of the survivors in the barn. But we all had the same things in common. All of us had lost our families and friends at the hands of the murderers. All of us had witnessed the worst atrocities done to mankind by the so-called most intellectual and most sophisticated nation of our time, the Germans. We would sit around and tell each other what each one of us had witnessed and how we had reacted to our experiences. It was good to see Srulki again.

Everybody looked sick, emaciated, dirty, and disheveled. There was a warm closeness among us but not a complete trust in each other. Our feelings of trusting another human had been completely shattered. But we were free to live. We were fed a minimum of what the Russian soldiers could spare, and we were guarded by them. But we were free to live.

One day I was sitting on the ground outside the barn, watching a Russian soldier eating his lunch, wishing I could be eating too. He saw me staring at him as he ate, and he decided to come over to me. He handed me his canteen filled with barley and potato soup and said, "Here, take it, little girl. This *menashka* [canteen] is filled with good soup, and I'm already full." I did not hesitate very long. I took the *menashka* and devoured the soup in no time at all. He stood there watching me, and I was embarrassed. I got on my hands and knees and went quickly to the well not far from us. I attached the *menashka* to the chain, lowered it into the well, and swished it around. Then I brought it up clean. I returned the *menashka* to the soldier and thanked him many times.

The next day the same soldier came looking for me with his soup. This time I took it and ate inside the barn, while he and other soldiers were watching the barn outside. After I finished eating the soup, I opened the back door and went to the well to wash his *menashka*. Inside the well, the *menashka* became detached, and I lost it. I was scared, and I cried all the way back to the barn. The soldier noticed me and asked why I was crying. I hesitated, then told him what had just happened to me.

"Do you hate me enough to want to shoot me with your rifle?" I asked.

He smiled and told me not to worry. Getting another *menashka* was no problem for him, he told me. Four more days I enjoyed his soup. Then his group moved on, and other Russians came and watched us.

One day my mother and two other women who survived from Goray received permission to travel to Goray. Mama and the others wanted to know more details about the fate of our loved ones. They wanted to inquire, from former neighbors and so-called friends, where and exactly how some of our relatives and friends had been murdered. The two other women who went with my mother were in their twenties. A Russian soldier escorted them to Goray in his jeep.

The first person Mama and the others saw when they arrived in Goray was Stefan Mrożyk. He was walking free in the streets of our town! Seeing this despicable murderer, who had terrorized the people in our hometown for several years, they became hysterical. The Russian wanted to know why they were so frantic about this man. So my mother and the other two women told the soldier about Mrożyk joining the Nazi Party during the German occupation and how he and his men had terrorized the Jewish people of Goray. They told how he and his gang had been responsible for the deaths of so many innocent men, women, and children and how he had had the Germans arrest many gentile people, and they too were sent to concentration camps, never to return.

Among the ones sent to camps was the priest from the big church. We later learned that the priest died from exhaustive interrogations. I remember the priest quite well. He was a very nice gentleman. The priest and Zlomainsky used to come over to our house. Together with my father, they would sip glasses of tea and eat cookies my mother baked. They would sit, sometimes for hours, discussing world affairs. All three agreed that Hitler and his Nazi Party must be defeated before they did much damage to the world.

Mr. Zlomainsky, the priest, and my father were good friends. Even though Mr. Zlomainsky and the priest were devout Catholics, and my father was a strictly observant orthodox Jew, they had a mutual respect for one another. Together they were striving for the world to become a better place for humanity to live in harmony. When it became clear that Germany was about to attack, the three of them would meet more often. When the Germans occupied Poland and their soldiers came marching in, their get-togethers stopped shortly thereafter. Gentiles and Jews were not allowed to mingle any longer, and Mrożyk and his men carried out those orders with pleasure.

The Russian soldier listened to my mother and the two other women. He told them to get a petition; all they needed were ten adults' signatures for the Russians to arrest Mrożyk.

Shortly after that, Mrożyk was jailed, and in the spring of 1945, he was hanged in the city of Lublin. My brother Josh was among those present at his execution. Thousands of people were present, mostly gentiles. These people came to see and enjoy Stefan Mrożyk getting what was due to him. The people, including my big brother, enjoyed their sweet revenge on that bright and clear day.

After we had spent three weeks in the barn, the gentiles were getting used to the idea that some Jews had survived and that we were trying to continue living in Bilgoray, at least until the war would be over. Mama found a small Jewish house, and ten of us survivors moved in. The house had three rooms and a kitchen with a woodburning stove. There was very little furniture in the house. The four of us shared one bed. We were cramped, but this was nothing new to us. No one complained.

At this point, Josh and I began to realize how much faster the others in the house got around. We were in pain. Our legs wouldn't straighten out, and crawling on the hard floors hurt and made us tired. Mama's concern about our not walking began to get on our nerves. "Why don't you two get up straight and walk like the others do?" Mama would repeatedly tell us. But we just could not do that.

My mother decided to take us to a doctor. After he had looked closely at us and examined us, his diagnosis was that we would never walk on our feet again. Having been in a fetal position for close to two years on cold and some days frozen ground, our muscles and nerves had grown together behind the knees. This was especially bad since we were still growing.

Mama couldn't accept what this doctor said, so she decided to take us to another doctor, Dr. Yablonsky, a so-called big specialist. Dr. Yablonsky's diagnosis was almost the same as the first doctor's, so Mama became very sad. "Don't worry, Mama," I said to her. "One day Josh and I will walk again like everyone else. We will also run, and we will even ride on a bicycle. You'll see, Mama. I promise!"

I was now eleven and a half, and Josh was fourteen, and we crawled like babies. We worked hard, trying again and again to hold onto chairs and to stand up. It caused a lot of pain, but it was beginning to work. We continued this painful exercise, the only remedy that Josh and I could believe in, and about a half year later we had become walking humans once again. Yes, we were on our feet and walking around, free to live! To be free to live is the greatest gift a person can possess.

We were free, but the war was not over. People were still tight with money and not very generous to others in dire need, such as Jewish refugees who had survived the German occupation in this area. My mother found a job in a restaurant in Bilgoray. She worked hard from early morning until late at night. For her labor, she received her food and the cold, cheap leftovers to take home for us, her children. Her legs would be swollen at the end of every day's work. Janice worked for a gentile family, cleaning their house and knitting sweaters for the children. For that she could eat her daily food. Josh and I were once again left alone all day. We were becoming a burden on Mama once again.

One day Mama heard about a Kinderheim (orphanage) in Lublin. She found out that in this orphanage they accepted children who had no mother and no father. Mama convinced Josh to travel to Lublin and register as one who had no mother or father. "Sometimes we have to tell a lie in order to live a little better," Mama told him.

About one month later, the Kinderheim had an open house for people to visit and see how the Communists took care of these orphans. Mama asked me to travel with her to Lublin to see Josh. I had a suspicion that Mama wanted to leave me there too. And I was right.

My first train ride was in a cattle car in which we could ride for free. The regular train cars were reserved for people who could buy a ticket. "We are lucky," said Mama, "that we can stand near the wall on this train." I held on to one of the boards and looked outside the train. I saw trees, houses, and children playing and laughing. But I was very sad to have to be away from my mother for the first time in my life. "It's only for a short time," Mama tried to reassure me.

The children were eating lunch when we arrived there. It smelled good. Josh's face and body had filled out, and he looked better. We didn't speak to him, so the leaders of this home wouldn't think we were related to him. He saw us, and he looked nervous. We walked outside, and Mama told me to go in and register. She said to me, "You'll have food and clothing, and you'll go to Polish school and learn to read and write. But do not mention me at all. You have nobody; you are all alone. That is what you will tell them." She kissed me quickly and walked away.

"What is your name?" a serious, stern face said to me. "Ah, ah, Helena," I answered. "Speak up, girl!" said this angry-looking woman. "Helena Rosenberg," I answered as loud as I could. I was very nervous and scared. "Where were you since *Judenrein?*" She looked straight at me and continued asking me many questions. I felt faint, and I wished my mother hadn't left me on my own.

In the orphanage in Lublin, we had food, clean clothes, and a bed to sleep in. We had teachers come to the home and teach us things. I was twelve years old when I began to learn the alphabet. In this *Kinderheim* of about a hundred children from infants to about age fifteen, we had all the bodily necessities. But I felt scared most of the time. What if they found out I had a mother? Or an older sister? Or that Josh was my brother? What if? What if? I constantly lived in fear. Josh and I met secretly. But the other children started a rumor that we were boyfriend and girlfriend, and they teased us endlessly. Josh was even more disturbed by all this than I was. So we decided to meet rarely.

I began to realize that on visiting days, people came from many different countries in the world, some even from America, to adopt a child or two from our orphanage. One day I saw an American in uniform with a woman, his wife, sitting and talking to little Sara, who was seven years old. They talked to her for a long time. Little Sara was crying, and then she was laughing, while the American couple were talking to her and holding her hands. We observers couldn't hear them, but we saw that after awhile they got up together with Sara, and as they walked by us, Sara said to us in Polish, "These are my new parents. They are taking me to America!"

We were all very envious of Sara. Most of the children adopted were the infants and the younger ones at first. Then, as time went on, older ones were also finding new parents. I must not forget that I had a mother. I had such mixed emotions. At first, I hoped I would be adopted and live in a normal home. But the thought of never seeing my mother again was just terrible.

As I became more relaxed in the Kinderheim and made friends, I found out that if any one of us had a relative, such as an aunt, uncle, or cousin, they could get a pass and go visit them. I gathered together my courage, went to the office, and told another lie. I said I had an aunt Esther in the city of Krashnik (where Mama and Janice now lived) and would like to see her. I received a pass and a train ticket to go. I was excited to see Mama and Janice. Krashnik had more than one hundred Jewish survivors by now, and more were trickling in all the time from the Partisans and those lucky enough to survive the death camps.

One day my mother met a woman who knew my sister Chaya-Leeba in the death camp Majdanek. For about three months, they would see each other in the field, doing hard, forced labor. Then one day in 1943, she no longer saw Chaya-Leeba. The woman didn't know whether Chaya-Leeba was sent to another camp or got sick and died or was gassed in the gas chamber, which was what she knew happened to most of the workers.

"Maybe Chaya-Leeba escaped?" asked Mama.

"I don't think so," answered the woman. "But there's always a rare chance that she may have."

Now my visits home were very tense. Mama only talked about Chaya-Leeba, hoping that one day soon she would show up. At night I would hear my mother getting out of bed, running to the door, and screeching, "I'm coming, I'm coming!" Janice and I would run over to her as she was unlocking the door and ask her what was going on. "Chaya-Leeba is at the door!" Mama would answer us and push us away so she could open the door for her. There was no Chaya-Leeba, of course.

Mama's dreams seemed very real to her, and she would run to that door in the middle of the night many times, only to be disappointed and sad. Chaya-Leeba never came back. But that one glimmer of hope lives with me even today. Whenever I attend survivors' gatherings, I always inquire and give them information about us. Whenever I meet a Polish Jewish survivor, I always inquire where she is from and what her name was before the war and during the war. Chaya-Leeba is most likely dead, but in my heart there is still a little spark that she's among us. I often fantasize about meeting and hugging my beautiful nineteen-year-old sister.

The leaders of the Kinderheim organized outings for us. We would go, usually on two buses, to museums and other educational places. We would sometimes stop in a field and have a picnic. We never knew where our next trip would take us. But that was always fun.

One day in the spring of 1945, we children from the Kinderheim rushed out to go on two buses, as usual, to some educational spot. The leader in each bus would usually announce to us, during our trip, where we were headed. On this day, our buses stopped about an hour after starting. Clara, our leader, announced to us that we had arrived in Majdanek, the liberated concentration and death camp. My heart skipped a beat when I heard the name Majdanek. We were all stunned. We all had many relatives and friends whom we had lost to the murderers here in Majdanek. No one moved when Clara ordered us to line up and get off the bus. She had to repeat herself several times before she got us to leave. I remember that as I stepped off the bus, human bone chips and ashes stuck to my shoes. The light rain that was falling made the ashes and bone chips moist.

"Those are your parents, sisters, brothers, and friends you are walking on," came a man's voice from a distance. "They were all shot or gassed to death, then burnt to ashes and bone chips," he continued in a loud voice. "Now all of you follow me," he said sternly.

There were about sixty of us from the two buses of children as well as other people, adults, in buses visiting Majdanek that day. We walked in silence, looking down, trying not to fall into some of the large piles of bone chips and ashes that lined the way until we arrived at a large building. We then stopped and listened to this harsh-sounding man telling us to follow him inside.

Inside, we walked through those unforgettable, morbid rooms, looking at thousand of shoes. Men's shoes, women's shoes, and tiny children's shoes. I remember catching sight of a black, shiny, patent leather shoe. My eyes couldn't move away from that shoe. I pictured my friend Yochi standing there in a pair of such shoes, and I saw her beautiful smile. I cried.

We moved on. There was lots of clothing, and there was human hair in bins against the wall. There were women's handbags on shelves, hair bands, belts, and so many other human accessories. Then I remember walking by several shelves on the wall, and there I saw human skulls. The man's voice came again: "These are the skulls that the German doctors admired. They thought these smooth, well-rounded skulls deserved to be on display."

I was getting very angry, very upset at the whole world – especially at this man. How could he talk about our loved ones in such a harsh and cold voice? I felt like running. But I didn't. I looked again at the skulls, wondering which one was my pretty sister, Chaya-Leeba. I stared and I cried. All these things and more were fenced off with wire fencing. We all stared in silence, and we all cried.

"Come this way," came the man's voice. He led us into a cold room with gray concrete walls. He ordered all sixty of us children, plus other visitors, to enter into this room. We complained and shouted, "There's no more standing-room in here!"

"Get closer to one another, more of you have to come in here!" he shouted.

We were practically standing on each other's feet, when we heard the huge metal doors slam closed, and someone on the outside locked them with an iron bar. We heard the bar fall in place. The man lifted his two flashlights to the ceiling, and he said, "You are now in a gas chamber. Those showerheads you see above you are not for water to wash up, as the people were told when they were given something resembling soap in order to fool them into this room. Those showerheads are connected to cans of Zyklon B gas above the ceiling."

"Oh, no! No, no, let us out of here!" people were screaming all around me. Someone screamed out, "This was all a plan to get us here and kill us with Zyklon B gas!" I was beyond panic. I felt faint – or was I dying from the gas? I fought that terrible feeling by telling myself, "It just isn't so. The war is over, and we are not going to die today, or ever!" I heard the man's voice again, "This gas choked your loved ones to death!"

We now heard someone lifting up the iron bar from the doors

outside. As the doors opened, we all stood there in deep shock. Some of the children had fainted, others threw up. Our teeth chattering, we all felt sick inside. We cried, we screamed, and we carried on for about ten minutes before we heard that man's voice again, "Follow me!"

"No more," we begged. "We can't take this any longer!"

"You can't take this? Well, you must!" said the man. "You are our future. You will have to tell the people all over the world what you saw here today. You will have to repeat this to the next generation. You will tell it all to your children and grandchildren some day. You will tell them about today and about everything else you've experienced. About all the atrocities that you saw and that you lived through. You will tell the world who did all these atrocities. It was the Germans, with the help of many other nations."

We followed the man. He opened a door and asked us to look inside and continue to walk so that others could see this room. Inside was a cement table and several stools around the table. The table was stained with human blood, and some human guts were on top of this table and on the floor. "This is where the villains opened the stomach of anyone they suspected might have swallowed gold or diamonds. This is also where they pulled out gold teeth from people's mouths," he said.

Next, he took us in the crematorium, where we saw three ovens on each side of a wall in the middle of the room. The oven doors were open, and halfway into the ovens were cement holders with wooden handles.

"This is where they burned our loved ones." This time the man spoke softly. "We lost millions of our people in many different ways. Most of them in places like this one," he said. "Don't ever forget your past as you go into the future," he said. "Now you know where those bone chips and ashes came from."

I looked down and saw my shoes. A bone chip was on one of them. I bent down. As I picked it up and looked it over very closely, I was wondering, "Could this be a part of my sister? Could this be Chaya-Leeba?"

Josh and I spent a little over one year in the *Kinderheim*. In December 1945 a Jewish Zionist group organized an exodus from Poland to West Germany, or the American Zone as it was then known, and Mama, Janice, and I were part of it. As Polish citizens, we had no right to leave Poland under the new Communist rule; therefore, it took us three full weeks to make it to West Germany. We would walk at night, and we crossed several borders of different countries, such as Czechoslovakia, Austria, and of course, the Polish border.

We were a group of about sixty people of all ages. I was among the youngest. We posed as Greeks going home after being deported by the Germans during the war. Before we reached each border, our two male leaders warned us not to talk at the checkpoints, where the Russian military inquired about us "Greeks" going home. When we were stopped, we held our breaths with fear, hoping we didn't have to turn back to Poland.

When we reached the border of West Germany, we were tired and even more frightened. What if the Russians realized we were Jewish refugees from Poland? After all, there were Jewish soldiers and officers in the Russian army. What if these Jewish men recognized us as Jews? They might take action against us. But the Russians and the Americans at the German borders were no fools. They knew, more or less, who these so-called Greek groups might really be.

As we reached the West German border, a few of the many Russians present decided to have some fun with us. "So, you are Greeks going home, eh?" said one Russian in uniform.

"Yes, yes, absolutely, we Greeks want to go home. Here are our documents," said one of our leaders, trembling a little.

"Well," said the Russian, "we have a Russian officer here who speaks fluent Greek. Would you like to talk in your mother tongue to this officer?" And before our leader could answer or say anything else, the Russian officer appeared. At this moment, you could have heard a pin drop. We were all in a panic.

"*Ma shlomchem, chaverim hayikarim?*" [How are you, my dear friends?] the Russian officer asked – in Hebrew! Our Zionist leader broke down and cried on hearing these Hebrew words. But he quickly composed himself, wiped his tears from his face, and answered the gentleman, also in Hebrew. "*Anachnu kulanu beseder, adoni. Todah rabah.*" [We are all very well, sir. Thank you very much.] The Russian Jewish officer then turned to his comrades and declared, "These people are really genuine Greeks. Let these people go." And away we went! Most of us recognized the Hebrew language, even though we really didn't understand the modern version. Oh, did it feel good to know that we still had some friends left in this world!

We arrived in the American Zone of occupied Germany without any further problem, and the Americans welcomed us. We came to a town called Funkasserne', near Munich. In the streets of Funkasserne', it was obvious that this was the American Zone; there were American soldiers everywhere. At first the men in uniform scared me, but I kept telling myself, "These are the good guys. They are here to protect us and to help us."

We were taken to some huge warehouses, where the men were housed in one building and the women in another. As Mama, Janice, and I entered the women's quarters, we were each given a pillow, a blanket, a towel, and a small bar of soap. Then an American volunteer lady showed us our three cots, with one little table next to the cots. I unwrapped the soap and made sure it was real. I couldn't help thinking of the gas chamber in Majdanek death camp, where the Nazis lured people in, giving them a bar of something that resembled soap, and made them think they were going in for cleansing.

The place we were in now was huge. There must have been hundreds of beds and night tables in this warehouse dormitory. During the day the men could come and spend time with their female relatives. My brother Josh had gone to the American Zone with a group of boys ages fifteen to eighteen two weeks before us. Boys that age traveled faster than did mixed groups. At this point, we really didn't know exactly where he was. But we knew he was safe.

The girl in the next cot across from mine was also twelve years old, and her name was Sonia. I made friends with Sonia almost immediately. She was there with her mother, grandmother, and eight-year-old sister Peppi. When meeting another refugee from Poland, the question was always the same: "Where were you after Judenrein?" She told me that the four of them, plus her father and grandfather, hid in a tunnel in the woods for two years. The adults took turns going out of this long tunnel at night to beg for food.

"So, your father and grandfather are in the men's warehouse?" I asked.

Sonia's eyes filled with tears, and very sadly she said, "No." She then told me that after two years of struggling to survive in this cold tunnel in the forest, her father and grandfather were killed by their former friends and neighbors, the gentiles of her hometown. They had gone back to their shtetl (village) near Lemberg, Poland, to ask the neighbors if they'd seen any one of their relatives alive since Judenrein and to ask for some of their belongings back. That's when the Poles killed them.

I hugged Sonia, trying to comfort her. She said she hoped we would be sent to the same DP (displaced persons) camp, so we could always be friends.

While Sonia and I were having this conversation, across from us sat a man and a woman on the woman's cot, talking. All of a sudden the woman, who was pregnant, started to scream. Then she fainted and fell to the floor. Sonia and I ran over to see if we could help her, as did others who saw her fall. As we stood there, the woman came to. We found out that her first husband had been taken to Majdanek death camp in 1942 and was never seen or heard from again by anybody who knew him, so he was thought of as dead. In May 1945 the woman had married her second husband, and they were now expecting a child. In the meantime, her first husband had somehow managed to escape Majdanek (an unusual occurrence) and had survived in the forest. When the woman saw her first husband walk through the doorway, she screamed and fainted. Later that day the woman and her two husbands left our dormitory accompanied by a volunteer, and we never learned the outcome of this interesting situation.

For two days Sonia and I were inseparable. Then she came to tell me that she, her mother, grandmother, and little sister Peppi were being sent to a DP camp called Föehrenwald. The name Föehren-wald didn't register with me. "I hope you will come there, too," she said. They took their belongings and left. Three days later, as the beds were being filled with new refugees and our dormitory was being guarded by the American military men, we were the next to leave. We received our first identification cards and were put on a bus to take us to the DP camp – at Föehrenwald!

During the war, Föehrenwald had been a training camp for German soldiers. This camp had many cottages. In most of these cottages there were three rooms, plus a toilet and small sink room, and a shower room with four showerheads. Each cottage had one large room upstairs and small and medium-sized rooms downstairs. The small rooms were given to couples with babies or young children. Mother, Janice, and I shared a medium-sized room with five other survivors, with eight people sleeping in four bunk-beds. We had an iron potbellied wood-burning stove in the middle of the room to keep us warm.

The camp was supported by the United Nations Refugee Relief Association (UNRRA), as well as by various American Jewish organizations, such as the Joint Distribution Committee, Organization for Educational Resources and Technological Training (ORT), and the Hebrew Immigration Aid Society (HIAS). Our food came mainly from America and included powdered milk and eggs, canned foods, and lots of ketchup. Used clothing, which also came from America, was distributed. There was a huge auditorium for Saturday night entertainment, such as movies from America. Sometimes a Yiddish film would be shown, and the auditorium would be packed. Sometimes a concert, with the camp's own musicians, provided the fun.

We also had a Hebrew Zionistic day school called Bet Sefer Tarbut B'Föehrenwald (Culture School of Föehrenwald). I went to this school for three full years, six days a week. The school had about 250 students, survivors from many European countries, speaking several different languages. Most of us did know some Yiddish. Of course, it was a pleasant surprise to find Sonia, whom I had met in Funkasserne'. Sonia and I became good friends. (She is now a grandmother and lives in the New York area with her family. We are still in touch.)

After six months of school in Föehrenwald, the faculty decided to make a new rule: all students must, from then on, speak only Hebrew in school. All our subjects were taught in Hebrew. When speaking to each other or to our teachers, "it must be Hebrew, or be silent." If the teachers heard us speak any other language, our grades would be reduced. At first it was hard for us students, so there was a lot of silence. But after a while we all began to speak, and we learned to be fluent.

Of course, we had English once a week as a foreign language. When the American committees would come to visit our classrooms, Mr. Grossman, our English teacher, would show off his good students. The Americans always had funny grins on their faces as they listened to Mr. Grossman and to us students. Not until I was in America for a while did I realize that Mr. Grossman and we, his students, all had heavy accents.

I find it hard to describe the first few months in Föehrenwald. It was as though we had been put on a dangerous planet, but we didn't care about the danger or have any other feelings inside us. We all knew we were living among the Germans and that among them there were the killers, the executioners of our loved ones – they didn't just disappear. On the other hand, we were fed, clothed, educated, and guarded by our friends, the Americans. Numbness – that is what we experienced at first. We, the people in the DP camp, would tell each other stories of our horrifying experiences without so much as shedding a tear. Our teachers asked us students to write about some of our experiences during the war. We wrote and handed over our stories to the teachers in silence, without emotions. My articles usually made it into our local newspapers. It didn't matter to me. I was numb.

Five thousand Jewish refugees came together in Föehrenwald. We were remnants from the harsh and bitter persecution. All of us were waiting for a country in the free world to let us in to live peacefully.

After six months in Germany, my sister Janice got married to a man she had befriended in the town of Krushnik, Poland. Janice moved to the city of Amberg, Germany, where her husband had rented an apartment. Now we had someone to visit in Amberg. By train, the trip took about an hour and a half because it made many stops. One of these stops was Nuremberg, where some of the notorious Nazi murderers were now standing trial. To us it was known as the Nuremberg Process. On my trips to Amberg, all I could think of as soon as the train started moving was Nuremberg and those killers. "Why do they give them a trial?" I thought. "What makes them entitled to have a lawyer on their side to defend them? Why not do what the Soviets did to Stefan Mrożyk?" (Three men tried, convicted, and executed him.)

I became angry on every trip to Amberg. As we got nearer to Nuremberg, my blood would begin to boil. Those calculating, cold-blooded, merciless murderers had followed a plan to humiliate, degrade, and systematically exterminate six million men, women, and children to make Europe *Judenrein*. These executioners were given a trial? Why? I felt such anger, such hate, during those moments that if given the chance, I would have smashed their skulls with my bare hands myself (or so I thought to myself).

I managed to hear the train conductor announce the stop after Nuremberg, which was called Schwandorf. I tried to compose myself in order to look normal to my sister and my new brother-in-law, Sam. These hateful thoughts inside me bothered me a lot. My father had taught us never to hate. "Hate only hurts the one who carries it inside," he would say. My father was no longer there to guide me. But I was smart enough to realize that one of the ways the enemy could win was by instilling hate inside me so that for the rest of my life I would only dwell in hate and never enjoy life. Oh, how I hated them for making me feel such hatred! I decided I would force myself to concentrate on pleasant things – good things to make me happy.

I used to enjoy my visits to my sister. I would sleep in a normal bed, get a glass of regular cow's milk, and sometimes have a hard-boiled egg to eat. One day while Janice and I were preparing some food in the kitchen, there was a knock on the door and two American soldiers came in. They each carried two packages of nylon stockings in one hand and three bars of Hershey's chocolate in the other, waving them at us. I became hysterically happy when I saw the nylons, and especially the chocolate bars. One soldier handed me the nylons and the chocolate, and then he hugged me. "Look, Janice," I said as I held up the goodies. "These American soldiers are even better than the Russian soldier who gave me his lunch every day for weeks. Look – chocolate, nylons, and he's so happy we survived the war that he's hugging me!"

"You let him hug you five more minutes, and he'll have sex with you!" Janice yelled at me. "Give him back the goodies and let's throw them out. They came for Helga and Gerta, who live one floor above us. They stopped in here by mistake." And she picked up a rolling pin and waved it at those two good-looking American soldiers.

She pointed her finger at the ceiling, yelling, "*Raus, raus, schweins!* [Get out, get out, you pigs!] Helga and Gerta are above!"

They started grabbing their candy and nylons back as Janice attacked them with the rolling pin. They just couldn't wait to get out of the apartment. As they were leaving, I ran over to my cute American. I pulled him by the back of his jacket, and as he turned around, I grabbed one bar of chocolate and one pair of nylon stockings out of his hands. Then I helped my sister push them out the door, and we locked it.

"Why did you take a bar of chocolate and a pair of nylons from them?" asked Janice.

"Why not?" I answered. "So what if Helga and Gerta will have one chocolate bar less and one pair of hose less. I love American chocolate, and Mama would never have enough money to buy me nylons. This way, I have both!"

"Don't ever do that again!" warned Janice.

"Why not?" I asked.

"It's stealing!" she answered.

In June 1947 my sister gave birth to a son. The new baby boy was very precious and very special to us, for he was the first addition to our small family – the first seedling budding among us. Life took on a new meaning to us. We all became a "somebody." I became an aunt, and Josh became an uncle, but most of all, Mama became a grandmother, a title she so loved.

Now more than ever, Mama was hoping that America would open her heart, open her doors, and take us in. As she used to say then, "America is a country where we can go to sleep at night and not worry that there will be a knock on the door, and the knock will be followed with an order, 'Raus Jude!' [Out, Jew!] There, in America, we can sleep peacefully," Mama would say.

In the summer of 1947 our whole school was sent to a camp sponsored by American Zionist organizations. The camp, called Camp Mittenwald, was in Bavaria, Germany. The name *Mittenwald*, literally translated, means "in the middle of the forest." We lived in tents, and we had fun. We were also being trained for *aliyah* (emigration) to the upcoming new state of Israel. There was a lot of talk about the United Nations creating a Jewish state in Palestine, where at that time, we were told, there were about six hundred thousand Jews and half a million Arabs living under the British Mandate. The Jewish people had been waiting, praying for a homeland for almost two thousand years. Could it really happen in my lifetime? A Jewish state? A country we could call our own? Could it really be that soon we would no longer be called "DP-niks"? I was overwhelmed.

In November 1947 the United Nations did vote to divide Palestine and create a Jewish country, and we became a Jewish nation called Israel in June 1948. There were celebrations: people were dancing in the streets; people were crying from joy that we had lived to be worthy of such an event. People were also crying from sorrow, knowing that six million of our people had to be murdered for the world to finally notice us, the few hundred thousand who survived. We, the refugees, who until now no country had wanted to take in, were like a thorn in their hands to be removed and put somewhere. We needed a place for the future generations of the survivors. We needed a homeland of our own.

In June 1948 the British pulled out of Palestine, and the Jewish state became a reality. No sooner did the British leave than the state of Israel was attacked by its neighbors, and there was a war. The Jews in the DP camps were worried and scared. Some of our young men of army age left for Israel to help in this war. Some were allowed to enter Israel; others were either sent back or put in concentration camps on Cyprus. And others were killed.

My brother Josh was now almost seventeen, and I was fourteen; we both wanted to go to Israel as soon as we could. We wanted to help win the war and be involved in building a Jewish state. We wanted to be among the *chalutzim* (pioneers). But Mama cried and said she wouldn't go along with our idea. Now that America was beginning to take in some refugees, Mama wanted to go there, where we had some distant relatives. At this point in our lives, Mama felt that every relative counted. She also felt that she had lost enough in wars. She said that she only wanted to live in peace and see her three remaining children grow up and give her grandchildren. In America, Mama felt, she could reach that goal.

And so I remember that on January 20, 1949, Mama and I were approaching the United States of America. Several hundred of us Jewish refugees stood on the deck of the boat, the Marina Marline.

"Look, Naomi," said my mother to me as I stood close to her at 5:30 A.M. My head was resting on her shoulder, her arm around me. "Look straight ahead at those beautiful lights in the distance. Those are the lights of New York. Those lights come from the city and country of our new home," said Mama. "In this new country, America, we will try to rebuild our lives and continue the future of our Jewish existence. You, Naomi, are young. You may manage to forget some of the horrors you have lived through and witnessed others go through."

"No, Mama!" I snapped at her. "I will never forget, nor will I forgive those responsible for the atrocities and humiliations they caused us and our loved ones, who are gone forever. If I forget all those dear people I knew, who were murdered in vain, they, the dead, would not forgive me. But the most important thing to me is, I would not forgive myself!"

Mama looked at me and said, "You always had a strong mind of your own – why should you change now?"

Six and a half hours later, at high noon on a crisp winter day, we were greeted by my mother's uncle, Charles Rubinstein, who had come to America many years before the war. By his side stood my brother Joshua, who had come to this country the year before as a student. We hugged and cried for a long time.

"I'm your uncle," said Charles Rubinstein, "and you are my only family, with the exception of my only son, who lives in the new State of Israel."

I hugged Uncle Rubinstein again, and I said to him, "We are very happy, and very grateful, to have you as our uncle." I wiped my tears, and I looked up at the clear sky.

I'm standing on top of the strongest foundation in the world, I thought. The United States of America, the land of liberty, the land where freedom belongs to everyone, and freedom is so easily being taken for granted. I'm standing on the soil of America, the land of my dreams. But I'm standing with a heavy heart and dragging along with me a heavy load of guilt.

I feel guilty that my parents had to care for me in such difficult times during the war years in the ghetto. I feel guilty that they had to always be alert and think of hiding me during the *akzias*, when Jewish children and old people were being caught and sent off on wagons to be shot to death and buried in mass graves. The guilty feeling is with me when I close my eyes, and I see my two little boy cousins' heads being chopped off with a hatchet by the terrorizing Germans, and I'm helpless to save them.

I feel guilty when I think of my friend Chana's blood on my hand as I picked up her head, and then I drop it right back down as I realize that Mrożyk the beast had just shot her, and I run away with all my might, straight home, as his bullets follow me and miss.

I feel guilty that the head of our family was so brutally put to death. My father was the crown of our "shining menorah." The Germans fooled us children by telling us that our father would be spared to live if we went to be with our mother in Frampol. Mama called us "crazy children." She said we should not have believed the Germans. They didn't tell the truth to Jewish children. Mama was right, I feel guilty and very sad.

I feel guilty for asking my sister Perele to slow down for me, so I could hold on to her coat pocket and not die alone. She got hit by a bullet in her leg from a German soldier, out on the field. She was bleeding so much. But she pushed me to get up and run fast, to catch up with Mama. "Maybe somebody will survive from our family to tell about these horrors," she said. "Maybe that somebody will be you."

My beautiful seventeen-year-old sister is shot, the world seems to be ending, I'm surrounded by corpses and wounded children, mothers, fathers, and others, on the plowed field, with the German army shooting at us. I'm only nine and a half years old! Why are they shooting at us? Why do they want to kill me so badly? What will they gain when I'm dead? I'm not the enemy. I have no territory they can take from me. And why am I running again, leaving my dear sister to die on the field, a slow, torturous death? Or be buried in a mass grave while she's still alive! Why?

The guilt is eating away at me for having caused Mama so much trouble, trying to hide out those last two years before we were liberated. "Children are nothing but trouble these days," whispered my brother Joshua to me during our hiding. Mama would have had a much easier time hiding out without three young children dragging along with her. But Mama never deserted us. She always came back to protect us. Mama also had a very hard time keeping us fed and dressed. It must have been very painful for Mama to watch my brother and me crawl like little animals after we were liberated. And for that I feel guilty.

Now, at age fifteen, I'm standing on the soil of the free and the brave, with my heavy heart and my bundle of guilt. I wipe my tears away again, and I look up to the clear blue sky. I stand here with such mixed emotions. But now is a time to be grateful and to think of good things ahead. Being outside, looking at the sky, makes me feel free. I whisper quietly to myself, "We are free. Free to live!"

Right: Mama, Faiga Rosenberg, in a DP camp, Camp Föehnenwald in West Germany, 1948.

Below: Mama; my brother, Joshua Rosenberg; and me in Poland, 1945.

Left: In a *Kinderheim* (orphanage) in Lublin, Poland, 1945. (I'm third from the left in the rear.)

Below: My sister Janice and brother, Joshua, in Poland, 1945.

Left: At a camp in Mittenwald, Germany, 1947. My friend Ester is on the right.

Below: My husband, me, and Srulki Citrinbaum (*right*), who hid with us for fifteen months at the Kowaliks. Photographed during our first visit to Israel, 1968.

Right: The Holocaust museum, Yad Vashem, in Jerusalem, Israel, 1994. The inscriptions bear testimony to the Jewish communities in Poland destroyed by the Nazis. Among those listed is my hometown of Goray (seven lines from the top).

8. At the wedding of my son Joey in 1996: *rear, left to right,* son Philip Samson, husband Harry Samson, me, daughter-in-law Linda Black-Samson, Joey Samson, son-in-law Jack Leeb; *front,* grandson Benjamin Samson, daughter-in-law Iris Samson, grandson Jeffrey Samson, daughter Sherry Leeb, grandson Michael Leeb. Grandson Marc Leeb, nine months old, not in photo.

Epilogue

When one of my sons was sixteen years old, I noticed one day that he was upset about something. He seemed troubled and tried to avoid me in order not to have to talk to me about his problem.

"Is something bothering you, son?" I asked him. "You seem sad about something. Would you like to talk about it? I'm here for you."

He looked at me, hesitated for a while, and then said, "Yes, Mom, something is bothering me, but I can't talk to you about it."

"Why not?" I asked.

"You see, Mom, next to what you endured during World War II, my problem will seem very trivial to you. I also don't want to upset you."

"But, son," I said, "I don't remember telling you, your sister, or your brother much about my past."

You see, Mom, there are several kids in my class in school whose parents are survivors of the Holocaust. When I visit my friends' homes, I hear their parents talk about the horrible and sad experiences that they lived through during the war as Jews in Europe. I know that you are also a survivor of the Holocaust; therefore, I know that you, too, must have had a painful and sad past."

I put my arms around my teenage son's shoulders, and I told him that in order to survive, I had to live through a few bitter years. I told my son that I happened to be born and have lived during the worst of times in history for the Jewish people in Europe and that I had wanted to live and survive so badly that I had no choice but to hide and live like an animal - or worse. But many years had passed since I became a free person, so now I considered myself quite normal - as normal as any other American woman. All the trivial things that bother others are also bothersome to me. "For instance," I said, "if I get a run in my stockings, I become upset like any other woman. When I see weeds on our lawn, I go bananas. What?! Dandelions? I must get rid of them immediately! And when I see a mouse these days, I really go crazy. Yes, son, I am human once again, and all these trivial things bother me too. Now tell me what it is that is bothering you."

"Mom," he said, "I think I'm in love with this great girl, but she doesn't really know it, and I don't quite know whether I should let her know how I feel about her or what else I should do about it." My son poured his heart out to me, and we talked for a long time.

My husband, Harry, and my three children, Sherry, Philip, and Joey, are my pride and joy. They are everything I ever wanted in a close-knit family. Having them is my best revenge against Hitlerism.

━━━

During the time we hid under Mrs. Kowalik's barns, when hope was only a tiny spark inside me and our minds and bodies were frail, one of the things that kept me going from day to day was a dream that someday we would be free and that we would make it all the way to America. I often used to fantasize: "I'm in America, the greatest country in the world. I'm standing on a bench, and many people come to hear me tell them my stories about what I experienced during this horrible war. I also tell the people what others went through, which I personally witnessed. I tell them the terrible things others had to endure and how, in the end, they were murdered." My dream was that the American people were eager to hear me out and they sympathized with me. They wanted to hear it all. In reality, it wasn't like that at all.

Whenever my mother would talk to her *Landsleit* (fellow countrymen) who had come to America many years before World War II and try to tell them about our suffering at the hands of the Nazis and the Polish anti-Semites, they asked Mama not to tell about so much tragedy. "It is hard to listen to such sadness," they told her.

For the first two and a half months in America, we lived in New York with my great-uncle Yitzchak Rosenberg and his wife, Aunt Freyda; their single son, Mickey; and their married daughter, Ethel, and her husband, Sam. Uncle and Aunt Rosenberg also had three married sons, Philip, Charles, and Hyman, who had served in the American armed forces during the war. Charles was on the front lines against Japan in the Pacific; Philip and Hyman had fought the Nazis in Germany. Now, in 1949, they were all back in the United States, and they all lived in New York. Uncle Yitzchak's family lived in a third-floor apartment on the lower east side of Manhattan. Uncle Charles Rubinstein (my mother's uncle) lived by himself in Bridgeport, Connecticut; his wife had passed away six months before we arrived in America.

Uncle and Aunt Rosenberg were very nice and very good to us. But they too told my mother not to talk too much about "those sad things," as they called our tragic experiences. Uncle and Aunt Rosenberg had many visitors coming to their home. Most of them came to see us, their "Greenie" relatives from Europe. These visitors repeatedly told my mother to stop telling her morbid stories. One man said to Mama, "Forget the past, be glad you survived, and don't make others sad with your morbid stories."

I absorbed it all, but my mother was upset with these people. "All they want to hear is good news, and have a good time!" she said.

One day my brother Josh was present when someone told Mama not to talk about "those sad things." Josh leaned over to Mama, who was sitting next to me, and whispered to her, "Mama, don't tell the people in America what we went through during the war in Europe. They don't want to hear it, and they don't want to know."

Right there and then, I made up my mind that I would work hard to disguise my identity. I wouldn't speak an English sentence – or even one word – unless I could pronounce it correctly. No one must ever know that I was a refugee of World War II.

After just three days in this country, I was enrolled in Suart Park High School on Essex Street. I tried hard to learn all I could, especially the English language. The kids in school were very nice to me. They helped me with my homework during lunchtime. When I came home, I had time to help Aunt Freyda with her housework.

One day when I came home from school to Aunt Freyda's apartment, she asked me to sit down at her kitchen table. She then brought over a Yiddish newspaper and put it on the table in front of me. "Can you read this paper, Naomi?" my aunt asked.

"Yes, Tante [Auntie]," I replied. "Not very fast, but I can read it. Why?"

"I envy you, Naomi," said my aunt. This little sixty-five-year-old woman, who was always so pleasant and always had a terrific sense of humor, was standing at her kitchen table almost in tears. "Naomi," she said, "I'm almost illiterate, and I don't like it. I can't read or write in any language at all. All I know is how to read from the Hebrew prayerbook, but I don't understand what I am reading. I know that I praise the Lord and ask him to forgive me for my sins. I pray to God to make our world a better place to live in." My aunt wiped her eyes as she was talking to me.

"But, Tante," I said, "what about the Yiddish letters I used to write to you and Uncle?"

"Oh, Naomi, your letters were just great. I used to take your letters with me to the synagogue on the Sabbath. There was a woman in the women's section who read Yiddish very well. Usually a group of women gathered around and loved to listen to your three- and four-page letters. They were always so informative, so refreshing, and often funny."

"But, Tante, who wrote the letters that we received back from you?" I asked.

"The same woman would come to my apartment during the weekdays. I dictated and she wrote."

"How interesting," I said.

"Interesting? You want to hear an interesting story, Naomi, then listen to this." Aunt Freyda sat down across the table from me and began telling me how she became a citizen of the United States of America.

"In a way," said Aunt Freyda, "it's a funny story now, but when it happened it wasn't funny at all to me." She continued, "I tried to go to night school to learn how to become a citizen. But between being a housewife, having several boarders in our apartment to attend to, and sewing clothes for people to help make ends meet, I really had very little time to study. I managed to learn a bit of history and something about our presidents, but not much else. I also learned to sign my name in English."

Tante then proceeded to tell me how she came before a judge. He asked all kinds of questions, but she didn't know the answers. "Something about, 'Who meets in a house of representatives? What are the kind of branches that are executive? Who makes up laws, and who interprets them?' How should I know these things? I'm just a simple woman who loves America and wants to become a citizen." Aunt Freyda continued, "When he asked me, 'Who was our first President?' I knew and told it to the judge. 'It was Judge Washington, and our present president is Truman.' Then he asked me, 'Who freed the slaves?' But when I answered him, 'It was Moses, who took out the Jewish slaves from Egypt,' the judge burst into laughter and told me he couldn't make me a citizen of this country I love so much.

"I became so upset at this judge, that I got his attention while he was wiping his glasses and still laughing, and I said to him, 'Listen to me, my dear judge. I've been in this country over thirty years. My husband and I have worked very hard to bring up five children – four sons and one daughter. We had to double up in our bedrooms at night, in order to accommodate several boarders for a very low rent. But it helped, and we managed. We gave all our children a good education. All of our sons graduated from college and have always been productive citizens in America. Now three of our sons are fighting and defending our beloved country. Two of our sons are fighting in Germany against our enemy Hitler and his Nazis. One of our sons, Charles, is defending this country against Japan. I hope and pray to God that one day soon, this terrible war will end, and our sons will all return healthy. And I will greet them not only with hugs and kisses, and with a bowl of chicken noodle soup, but also with great pride in myself, telling them that I, their mother, am now an American citizen. So, dear judge, don't turn away from me, and don't take away what is so dear to me, to become a citizen of the United States of America. Please don't kill my dream!'

"The judge looked down over his desk and called me over closer to him. Then he said to me, 'Mrs. Rosenberg, you are a special lady, and I am going to make you an American citizen, just sign here.' I signed, and he shook my hand and congratulated me. That is how I became a citizen."

I gave my aunt a hug and told her what an interesting story she had just told me. Then I asked her, "Would you also like to be able to read this Yiddish newspaper?"

"Would I!" she chuckled.

"You can, Tante," I said to her as I pulled her over to sit right next to me.

"How?" she asked.

"I will teach you," I said. "You already know all the Hebrew letters. The *Alef-Bet* (ABCs) is the same in Yiddish as it is in Hebrew; they just sound somewhat different. I will teach you to put the *Alef-Bet* together in Yiddish right from the newspapers in less than six months. You can manage to spare a half hour every day in order to be able to read a paper. Right?" She looked at me with a smile and her mouth open. "Now, let's begin," I said.

"But I have to make supper," said Aunt Freyda.

"Tante," I said sternly, while holding her hand, "if you are serious about learning to read, let's begin now!"

For the next five months, I would arrive at Aunt Freyda's house and find her sitting at her kitchen table at the same time, with a Yiddish paper in front of her, very eager to begin another lesson. Needless to say, after five months she was reading the Yiddish paper faster than I could. She was so proud of herself – and so was I!

It felt good to have relatives once again. I enjoyed walking home from school, not rushing. I looked in the windows of all the stores along the way home. I especially loved looking into the produce stores. I just couldn't get over the fact that the price of an orange and the price of a large potato were about the same. As a little girl in my hometown, I would get an orange maybe twice a year. But potatoes – everybody grew them. Until the war years, I never went hungry for potatoes or other "normal" foods. But oranges, that was a luxury! I saved some of my lunch money and bought at least one or two oranges every day on the way home from school. I was also curious enough to look inside bars and see men drinking beer and watching tiny television screens. All I could see on the TV was boxing, and that was a disappointment to me. Then I discovered Tuesday evenings, when Milton Berle was on.

I loved Saturday nights in the winter, when all of Uncle Yitzchak's children came to visit and brought their friends, mostly young men who had also served and fought the enemies during the war years. We all sat around Aunt Freyda's big table in her large kitchen. We'd have refreshments and interesting conversation. Most of the time, the guys talked about their experiences in the military. I enjoyed listening to their heroic stories of the war. Charles's stories about Japan sounded quite different from the stories that the others were telling about the war with Germany, which were more familiar to me. They were a good group. They talked, they laughed, and sometimes they would cry, remembering a buddy who didn't make it home. They cried over a particular friend whose guts were spilled on the field, shot and killed fighting for his country, the great United States of America, just days before the fighting ended. They cried remembering how they carried a close friend who was shot on a stretcher for a long time, then he just closed his eyes and died. I cried too, remembering my friends and loved ones who were so brutally murdered. They weren't killed fighting the enemy; they were murdered for having been Jewish. Sometimes it became sad on Saturday night in uncle and aunt's kitchen. Then someone would raise a glass of whiskey, and a toast would be made. Someone would say, "May our children never know war!" or "Cheers!" or "L'Chayim! [To life!] And to happy days ahead!" Once again, all were in a good mood.

In April 1949 Mama and I rented our own small apartment five blocks from our aunt and uncle's house. Mama got a job in the garment industry hemming dresses, working eight hours a day, five days a week. She worked standing on her feet, not being allowed to sit down. They paid her twenty-seven dollars a week, but it just wasn't enough to pay rent and cover our other necessities. So I started night school, and my cousin Hyman helped me get a day job in the jewelry factory where he worked. He was a solderer, using a gas blowtorch to solder together links of costume jewelry. I was a beginner in the impressions and layout department.

Cousin Hyman warned me that my foreman, Frank, was an anti-Semite, and that no Jewish woman ever lasted in his department more than a few weeks at the most. But jobs were hard to come by, especially for a beginner at age sixteen without any experience. Frank the foreman did try to make my life difficult so that I would quit. He made me cut metal chains by hand, while others did it by machine. He put me in a corner at a small table so that I couldn't talk to anyone and felt isolated. He also removed the light over my table, telling me it had to be fixed, so I was forced to work without much light. At the end of each day, I went home with blisters on my hands. My hands would bleed and be painful.

But what Frank the foreman didn't know was that I, Naomi Rosenberg, wouldn't quit just because of painful hands. With bandages and thin gloves on my hands, I continued to work until one day one of the bosses noticed me and asked what was going on. I was then put back with the other people in the regular department, and I began to learn how costume jewelry was made. A year and a half later, I was made a foreman, and my salary was raised substantially. There were fourteen women in my department from all walks of life. We all got along well. My department became very efficient and productive; therefore, I had some extra time to start working on my own designs. My bosses liked some of the pins, earrings, bracelets, and necklaces that I designed, and they paid me extra for each piece they accepted for production.

As soon as we earned a few dollars, Mama started campaigning to send help back to our rescuers in Poland. "We must not forget the Kowaliks," she would say. She asked neighbors and relatives to give her some used clothing, children's clothes and shoes, and other items. She would also talk me into giving up some of my blouses and skirts. At the time, I didn't have many things, but Mama scolded me for even trying not to pitch in. And so we started making packages and mailing them to Poland.

Mama also wrote to Mr. Zlomainsky and asked what we could do for him. Mr. Zlomainsky answered that we should not send him anything at all because he didn't need material things. He said we should send Maria Kowalik and her seven children whatever we could, because things like clothing were expensive in Poland. In their letters, the Kowaliks seemed very happy every time they received a package from us. "We must send Stashek the bicycle that we promised him," I said. My mother ordered all of us to pitch in, and she attended to Stashek's bicycle. Of course, we sent Olesh his *bzytef* (shaving kit), and we sent *bzytefs* to the other Kowalik boys. My mother did most of the corresponding with Mr. Zlomainsky and the Kowaliks, with some help from my sister Janice. Mama and Janice were the only ones who could read and write Polish fluently.

In the mid-1950s Mama received a letter from one of the Kowalik children, saying that their mother's heart condition had become worse but that penicillin would help her get better. Once again my mother's courageous efforts paid off. She went to many doctors and was always turned away when she explained about the penicillin, until she found Dr. K. He really tuned in and listened to my mother's request, and he gave her as many prescriptions as necessary. In those days penicillin was fairly new and quite expensive. Mama spent every spare penny she had, and we pitched in too, so that penicillin was mailed regularly to Maria Kowalik in Poland. But sadly, in 1958 Maria Kowalik passed away.

We continued sending packages to the Kowaliks. After I got married and moved to Baltimore, I sent things to the Kowaliks on my own. They always acknowledged receiving my packages with great pride.

The only member of the Kowalik family interested in coming to America was Yanek, the oldest son. Since my husband, Harry, was in business, he arranged to send Yanek a visa to come to the United States. But before he could come, Yanek got sick. He was one of the last people to get polio. He became paralyzed, and he never made it to America. Mr. Saverek Zlomainsky passed away in 1960. We were very sad to lose such a humanitarian giant.

In the summer of 1950, my mother met and married a nice gentleman by the name of Isaac Sorgen. He was known to my sister, my brother, and me as "Uncle Isaac."

My sister Janice, her husband, Sam, and their two-year-old son, Izzy, came from Germany to the United States in July 1949. My brother Josh, who came to the States as a student the year before Mama and I arrived, was now graduating from high school with honors and had a full four-year scholarship to Davis and Elkins College in West Virginia. I continued going to night school and working as a jeweler. The people I worked with were all nice and friendly. My employers and I had a good rapport.

After working for about four years, I came in one day in June 1953 flaunting an engagement ring. "What is this?" asked one of my three bosses. "We knew you were dating, but engaged? Who is this guy, anyway?"

"His name is Harry Samson and he lives in Baltimore," I replied.

"Baltimore? Does that mean you will move to Baltimore and leave us?"

"Correct," I answered.

"You know, Naomi, we were planning to give you a very nice raise real soon. We were also going to pay you more for your designs. You are getting really good at it," said another employer. "Won't you stay, Naomi?"

"Nope," I answered.

"What is so special about this Harry Samson? Can't you find someone like him right here in our cosmopolitan city of New York? Why Harry Samson? Why him?"

"Harry Samson made me an offer I couldn't refuse," I said.

"And what might that be?" I was asked.

"He promised to love me unconditionally for the rest of our lives," I replied.

"What does he do?" "What is he like?" "Will he appreciate you and be good for you?" All these questions and more came from my employers. It felt good to see how much they cared and how much they needed me.

"To answer some of your questions," I said, "he is an architect and a builder. He is kind, gentle, caring, nice-looking, bright, and educated. He graduated from Yeshiva University and Columbia University School of Architecture. And he has a nice smile! After knowing him for about a year, I completely trust him. When I'm with him I feel good about myself."

"Okay. But do you love him?" came the final question.

"What do you think?" I answered.

I was nervous the first time I met Harry's family in Baltimore, especially when I found out that Harry's father was a rabbi and the dean of a Hebrew day school. When I arrived in their home, I was pleasantly surprised by the warm welcome I received from Harry's parents. I also met Harry's three sisters, Miriam, Rachel, and Rebecca. They made me feel at home. The Samson home had a very relaxed atmosphere.

Later on, Harry's sisters became not only family to me but also dear friends. I remember also meeting Harry's older brother, Norman, who was in the construction business with him. He seemed nice. I later learned that Norman had been a rabbinical student when the war broke out between the United States and Japan and Germany. Norman voluntarily enlisted in the U.S. Army and served under General Patton. He served until the war ended in 1945. In 1947 Norman went to Palestine to study at the Hebrew University in Jerusalem under the GI Bill. But when Israel was declared a Jewish State in 1948 and was attacked by its neighbors, Norman enlisted in the Haganah (the Israeli army) and fought in Jerusalem.

Harry and I were married on November 22, 1953, and I moved to Baltimore. About a year and a half later, I gave birth to our first child, a daughter. She was precious, and she was beautiful. Holding her in my arms and looking at her, I had a wonderful feeling inside. "She is completely dependent on me and her Daddy," I thought. I promised her that her Daddy and I would always be there for her, as long as she needed us. We named our daughter Shaindel, after my grandmother on my mother's side. We call her Sherry.

Although I was happy, every now and then a flashback would make me sad and scared. Sometimes, remembering what happened to Jewish babies during World War II in Europe, panic would overtake me. I pushed the sad thoughts out of my mind, as I had pushed out many other bad memories of the war years.

Two years later our son Philip was born, a joy to hold and to care for. His Jewish name is Pinchas, after my father. Dad was a very special person, and Philip is very special to us.

Our family was growing, but it did not feel complete until our youngest son, Joey, was born, on a bright and sunny Saturday morning three years after Philip. I held him close to me as I had held his sister and his brother before him. Another precious human being in our family. We named him Joseph after my grandfather on my father's side. He was a loving baby, cute and smart. There was a lot of pleasure in the house that Harry had designed and built for our now complete and happy family. We cared for our young ones, we played with them, read books to them, took them places, and did everything a normal American family did.

Inside me, though, there was little Naomi, pulling the strings, reminding me, through flashbacks, of the bad times. Little Naomi desperately wanted to come out, to tell the whole story, and to cry. But the grown-up Naomi would say, "No, you can't make people sad. Anyway, people still don't want to hear about it. So stay down, little kid. Don't rock the boat. Go back and hide." So I was trying to act normal, but it was getting harder all the time. The bubble inside me was growing bigger and bigger.

I had nightmares. In my nightmares, I ran, I hid, I was being chased by beastly looking uniformed men about to shoot me. I would be awakened by my husband. "You cried in your sleep, honey. What did you dream about?" Harry asked me on several such nights. I would tell him my nightmares. He would listen and cry with me.

In my nightmares I would also crawl on my stomach as somebody was pulling my knees. I would dream that people were laughing as I was crawling and trying to reach my mother's hand. I would almost reach her hand, but the mocking laughter made me pull back. I never would get to touch her hand.

My nightmares also involved my present house. In my dreams, it was surrounded by German men in uniform, all pointing their machine guns and rifles at my children and me, while I was crawling toward a light switch. In my hysterical nightmare, I felt that if I could crawl over to the wall and switch on a light, they would all disappear. But I never quite made it to turn on the switch. I'd be awakened by my husband; I would tell him my nightmares, and he'd cry again and again. We both cried.

After a while, Harry still woke me from my crying in my sleep, but he wouldn't ask what I dreamed about. It was obvious he couldn't deal with my pain at night. That was when I decided not to talk to him after he'd wake me. I didn't want to make him sad anymore.

I felt alone at times, as though I were hiding. "No one must know that I am a refugee of World War II. No one must find out I'm a Holocaust survivor. My English is pretty good. I'm careful not to say words I can't pronounce well. I dress nicely, and I try to look like an American."

I went on fooling the world around me, or so I thought. The only one I couldn't fool was myself. I became more and more depressed; I had fears that I couldn't understand. I was anxious, tensed-up. My nightmares became more and more frequent, and I still didn't talk about them. Some nights I woke up and automatically ran to see if my children were in their beds. At times life had no meaning. That really scared me, remembering that life had always been so precious to me. "Life is a gift from God, not to be taken for granted," I recalled my father saying.

In the mid-1960s, I confided in our family physician a little about my emotional state. He listened and suggested that I seek professional counseling. He gave me the name of a psychiatrist and recommended that I go see him. I felt I must get help. Harry agreed with me. He confessed that he found it very difficult to listen to my painful past. He felt that he was too close to me, and therefore it also affected him.

"Who are you, and why are you here in my office today?" asked Dr. G. His stern voice scared me. I just wanted to curl up and disappear. My palms were sweating; I didn't know what to do with my hands, but I began to talk.

"Well, you see, I'm Jewish, and I'm one of Hitler's leftover children, that he didn't quite get to kill. During the war I had to run, and I had to hide from the Nazis in Poland and ..."

"Stop, young lady," I heard him say to me. "The world has heard enough about it, and so have I," he continued. "Living through a war makes people stronger. They can endure more than those who never saw war. Soldiers come back from wars and from war prisons, and their emotions are much better than those who didn't serve their country. So don't tell me about the past war years. Tell me about now, and what is bothering and disturbing you now."

I looked at this man, Dr. G., and I saw him as an SS man in uniform with a gun on his hip, a rifle on his shoulder, a rubber hose in one hand, and a hatchet in the other – Judenfarnichters (destroyers of the Jews), as they were known to be. That is how I saw Dr. G. I felt trapped. I couldn't wait for the end of this session. Dr. G. set me back quite a lot. I continued to hide my past, my childhood of fear and anger. The bubble inside me felt like it was exploding.

One day my brother Josh came to spend a weekend with us. Josh, by this time, was a psychologist. He had recently finished four years of Ph.D. work at the New School for Social Studies in New York. I talked to him about my problems and about Dr. G. Josh told me I had picked the wrong man to help me. He reminded me that, as children, we had experienced many great traumas during the war years. He advised me to seek professional help through an organization or agency that was familiar with survivors of the Holocaust. He told me to pick someone I liked talking to and whom I felt I could trust.

Mrs. Weinberger, the executive director of the Baltimore HIAS, came to mind. She had been very understanding and gentle with me when she interviewed me during my application for restitution money from the German government. Mrs. Weinberger referred me to Dr. R., and I began to see him once a week.

For several weeks I hardly said anything, still afraid he would start talking the way Dr. G. had. But this man was kind and gentle. He asked questions, and I answered with a "Yes" or a "No." Whenever I raised my head, he stared at me and said, "Say it, Mrs. Samson, say whatever comes to mind." I looked at my watch, then turned my head away. "What was it like for you as a young girl in Poland under the Nazi regime?" he asked me one day.

I kind of liked Dr. R., so I pitied him, because I didn't want to upset him or make him sad. And I told him that. He told me not to worry about him; he said he could take care of himself. He also explained to me that he had been trained to listen to anything anyone would say. He promised me that if he couldn't take it, he would let me know. "Go ahead, Mrs. Samson. Take a chance. Say whatever you are thinking about right now."

I closed my eyes. For a while I was quiet. Then I began to sob. Tears flowed down my face onto my hands. He handed me a box of tissues. I wiped my eyes, but my tears didn't stop falling. My eyes closed, and I began to talk. I talked and I cried continuously. My mind was thousands of miles from where I was sitting, describing my childhood and those horrors I had lived through.

"Mrs. Samson, Mrs. Samson," I heard Dr. R.'s voice. "I'm sorry to have to interrupt, but our time is up. We'll continue next week." I opened my eyes slowly and tried to compose myself, but the flow of tears was continuing nonstop.

"I feel as if I climbed mountains. I'm exhausted, Dr. R.," I said.

"You did climb mountains, and you worked very hard, Mrs. Samson, and for that I congratulate you," he replied.

I walked into the bathroom, and Dr. R. called in his next patient.

I washed my face and looked in the mirror. My eyes were red and wet from crying. I walked to my car still crying. I drove home crying, wiping my eyes frequently in order to see the road and traffic. As I was driving, I remembered it was my carpool day; I had to pick up six children, including our three precious ones, from two different schools. I put on my sunglasses and made myself hum a happy popular tune in order to divert my thoughts and stop my crying.

The smiling faces of the children as they all climbed in my car, all six of them talking and giggling at the same time, made me think to myself, "Isn't it a wonderful world? Children laughing, teasing one another about the most trivial things, and I'm called 'Mommy!'"

I continued with Dr. R. for several years. It was tough, it was draining, but it was definitely therapeutic. Why did it help? At first I didn't understand. When psychotherapy was first suggested to me, I wondered, "How can it help? The therapist isn't going to bring back my loved ones. Nor can a therapist undo the suffering I endured. He certainly can't bring back the normal and happy childhood I was deprived of. I was a happy kid growing up in Goray. All of a sudden, my world was destroyed. Why even bother with therapy?"

In time I began to realize that therapy, for me, was like attending a great but very rigorous private school. I was learning so much at every session, and the subject was most interesting. The subject was *me*. To learn about oneself and to learn how to live and deal with a traumatic past; to unravel feelings like guilt, neglect, hate, and other such feelings; then, to learn how to overcome these terrible feelings that lived within me – that, to me, was a good school. I came to learn that we can never bring back the past or undo anything from the days gone by. But we can begin to appreciate today. We can learn to live and deal with the present, making the best of the years we have left on this earth. If we, the Holocaust survivors, don't do that, then Hitler has won.

――――

Our children were growing up, becoming smarter and more intelligent all the time. Our daughter, Sherry, and our sons, Philip and Joey, after attending Hebrew day schools from grades 1 through 12, all graduated from universities and received postgraduate degrees.

As time went on, one by one our children got married and built their own families. First, Philip married his college sweetheart, the intelligent, caring, and pretty Iris Gross. Together they created two wonderful sons: Benjamin was our firstborn grandchild; his brother, Jeffrey, came three years later. They are great and loving grandsons. Our beautiful daughter, Sherry, found the man of her dreams, the goodhearted, bright, intelligent, and handsome Jack Leeb. Together they produced Michael and Marc, their two sons, who are a joy to behold. Our youngest son, Joey, met, wooed, and wedded his precious, kind, and beautiful Linda Black in 1996.

To see our grandchildren play and laugh is always my greatest revenge against the Nazis. Today, Jewish children are free, like all children. They can learn about their roots and their rich heritage, and they are proud to be who they are. That is another way I enjoy my revenge against those who came close to annihilating us. I hope that someday, maybe in my lifetime, there will be a candle lit in many households honoring the memory of the more than one million innocent children who were so brutally murdered only because they were born Jewish. Jewish people have every reason to be proud. We made great contributions to the betterment of the world. We have always been a civilized people. We are known as "the people of the Book."

In my lifetime, I have lived through the worst of times that a child, or even an adult, can endure. But I have also lived to see the long-awaited creation of a Jewish state, the state of Israel. For thousands of years, the Jewish people were wanderers throughout the world. We were a people without a homeland. Today, we are a nation, with a country we can call our own. We are a free people.

No more running, no more hiding for me and for all Jewish children. Yes, we are free to live. That is definitely my greatest revenge against all Nazis in the world.

Surrounded by our children, our grandchildren, and some close friends, Harry and I celebrated our fortieth wedding anniversary in 1993. Each of our children made a speech. They each expressed their feelings and their gratitude to their father and to me. They were great, and we all applauded them. Then our grandchildren climbed on chairs and sang to us:

I love you, you love me.
We're a happy family . . .